JOHN WAYNE

★ MADE IN ★

AMERICA

AMERICA HAS BEEN BLESSED WITH MORE THAN HER FAIR SHARE OF OUTSTANDING CITIZENS THROUGHOUT THE COUNTRY'S HISTORY,

but no individual better embodies the Land of the Free than John Wayne. The grit, strength, determination and courage he displays in his movies made him an American icon—one still instantly recognizable around the globe to this day. But if you look beyond Duke's films, you'll also discover a life whose arc mirrors the story of our great nation. From his roots as a Midwestern boy who pulled himself up by the bootstraps to break into the fledgling film industry to a family man enjoying his well-earned prosperity in the postwar period, to standing up for patriotism in his golden years, John Wayne's story is the story of America. The following pages trace these two histories side by side, examining the ways John Wayne's past is inseparable from the history of the country he held so dear.

—ETHAN WAYNE

★ CONTENTS ★

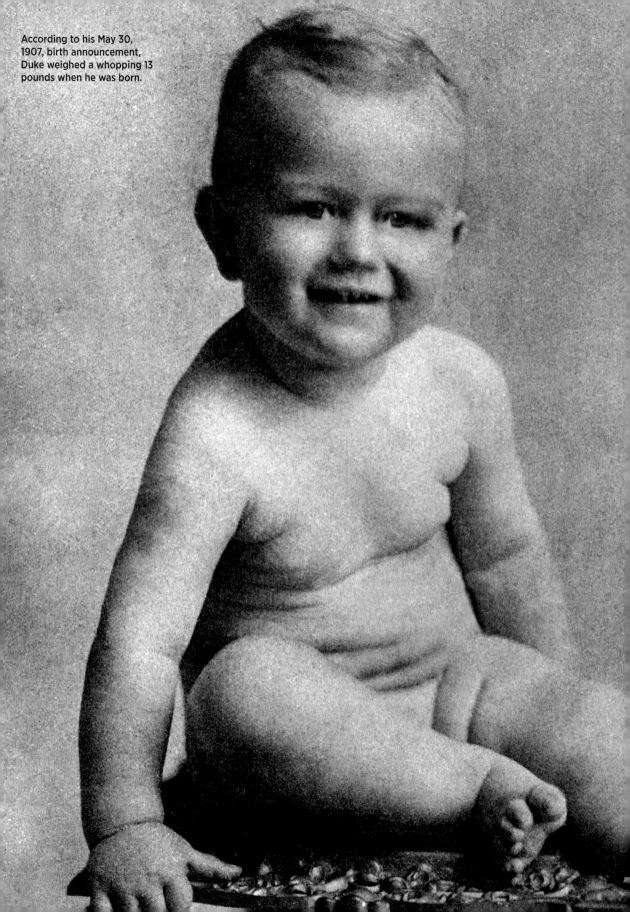

According to his May 30, 1907, birth announcement, Duke weighed a whopping 13 pounds when he was born.

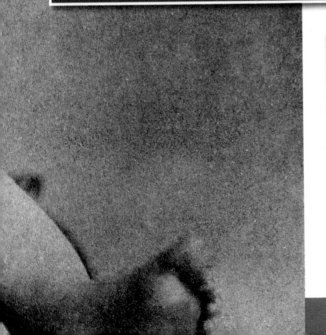

★ 1907–1925 ★
AMERICAN BOY

J OHN WAYNE was born in 1907, just as what was once called the "Wild West" was taking its last strides toward a more settled way of life. Duke may have helped shape what most Americans picture in their minds when they imagine the Old West—a world where civilization was never more than a bad day away from dissolving into anarchy, and where the law of the land mattered less than the speed of a gunfighter's draw—but John Wayne, then Marion Morrison, belonged to a generation benefiting from the sacrifices

The Last Spike, an 1881 painting by Thomas Hill, depicts the completion of the cross-country railroad.

made by the men and women who sweat, bled and died to settle the territory.

The changes Duke would live through, and eventually see the benefits of as a grown man, had begun during the presidency of Abraham Lincoln, who helped revolutionize travel to the West when he signed the Pacific Railroad Act in 1862. Although the fate of the country was still in doubt as the Civil War raged, Lincoln had the foresight to approve a project allowing travelers to venture as far as the Pacific Ocean without risking life and limb on an arduous, months-long journey. Under the terms of the act, the Central Pacific Railroad Company would start laying track from Sacramento, California, while Union Pacific Rail would begin from Omaha, Nebraska. The construction lasted seven years and took an incalculable toll on the thousands of workers employed in the project. But its consequence, the easy transport of goods and people from coast to coast, was nothing short of the realization of Manifest Destiny.

Before long, the stagecoach and the pony express rider would be replaced by the sleeper car and the telegraph wire, but the West remained a shining beacon of new opportunity well into the early 20th century. California, the state Duke would call home for most of his life, was becoming more and more important beyond its natural resources, and western migration would soon affect the most important new business in the country, defining John Wayne's future career. In 1905, the first nickelodeon (a portmanteau of "nickel," for the usual cost of admission, and "odeon," the ancient Greek word for roofed theater) opened in Pittsburgh, Pennsylvania.

Nickelodeons generally showed one- and two-reel films, with screenings lasting anywhere between 15 minutes to an hour and accompanied by piano music. The idea proved popular: Just two years later, approximately two million Americans had been to a nickelodeon, and by 1910 there were nearly 10,000 of these theaters throughout the United States, provoking the ever-increasing demand for silent films and making it clear there was a market for an entire film industry.

During this time, many filmmakers operated at the pleasure of Thomas Edison, inventor of the light bulb, phonograph and Kinetoscope (an early iteration of the movie camera). At the turn of the 20th century, Edison held most of the patents to the technologies needed to make movies. Together with other film-related patent holders, he helped form the Motion Picture Patents Company (MPPC) in 1908, which operated in New Jersey and controlled almost everything regarding film, from production to distribution to exhibition. The MPPC made it extremely difficult for filmmakers to operate without

Edison Kinetoscopic Record of a Sneeze
Taken & Copyrighted by W.K.L.Dickson
Orange N.J. — Jan. 7th 94

Stills from the earliest-surviving motion picture, recorded on Thomas Edison's Kinetoscope, "Fred Ott's Sneeze," c. 1894.

their permission, suing for unauthorized use of cameras and other equipment.

To avoid harassment by Edison, many filmmakers chose to set up shop on the opposite side of the country. Southern California was already appealing to filmmakers: The location was ideal, with a wide variety of landscapes from mountains to sea coasts to deserts within a 50-mile radius; good weather made it easy to produce movies year round; Los Angeles was already considered a home to professional theatrics; and land in

Hollywood was cheap and abundant. The silent films produced in Hollywood during the early 20th century defined what would become the American movie industry to the extent that, by the time war-weary GIs began returning home from World War I, it was to this new movie mecca they turned for a fresh start. The conflict that defined the 1910s left an entire generation scarred and broken, making the escapism of the movies ever more important. With Hollywood's help and with John Wayne waiting in the wings, the 1920s were ready to roar.

Humble Beginnings

Just before the clock struck 10 a.m. on May 26, 1907, a legend was born in a small town in Iowa. Proud parents Clyde Leonard Morrison and Mary "Molly" Brown welcomed their first child, 13-pound Marion Morrison. He would soon grow into a star student, a promising athlete and a winning personality, attributes that would serve him well on his rise to stardom.

When Marion was 4 years old, the Morrisons, along with new baby brother, Robert, left their home in Iowa and headed west to California. Clyde's tuberculosis required an arid climate, and so the Morrison patriarch briefly planted his family on a farm in the Mojave Desert. There, he would attempt to support his wife and two sons as a homesteader.

Life on the farm proved to be an education in hard living for young Marion and the rest of the family. The luxury of indoor plumbing was replaced with a hastily built outhouse, for example,

Marion Morrison (left) with his younger brother Robert.

A young Duke Morrison (left) with his baby brother, Robert, and their mother, Molly. Both Robert and Molly would pass away in 1970.

Duke and Robert with one of the family's dogs.

and Marion had to acquaint himself with unfamiliar chores such as killing rattlesnakes on the property. As Duke later told biographer Maurice Zolotow: "Seems to me like there musta' been millions. The more you killed, the more they kept on comin'...Shooting those snakes also gave me some sleepless nights—visions of thousands of slithering snakes coming after me. I used to wake up in a cold sweat in the middle of the night, but my dad, or my family, never knew it. I kept my fears to myself." Of course, John Wayne would later famously assert "Courage is being scared to death, and saddling up anyway," and Duke never shirked from his duties.

His chores weren't always so horrific, but they were plentiful and laborious, requiring Marion to get up before dawn to finish them before heading off for his lessons at Lancaster Grammar School, eight miles away from home. His preferred mode of transportation was a pony named Jenny, the first of many steeds Duke would rely on in his life. Taking care of Jenny, in addition to his other duties on the farm, helped instill in Duke a sense of responsibility that far outstripped his 8 years of age. Even at the height of his celebrity and influence in Hollywood, Duke was noted as being the first on the set and often the last to leave, no doubt thanks to the work ethic he developed during his years on the Mojave farm.

After failing to coax a cash crop from the unwelcoming land, young Morrison's father moved the family to Glendale, California, where he would return to his original vocation as a pharmacist. Despite their struggles, Molly

TAKING CARE OF JENNY... HELPED INSTILL IN DUKE A SENSE OF RESPONSIBILITY THAT FAR OUTSTRIPPED HIS 8 YEARS OF AGE.

maintained her go-getting spirit and made sure her boys were always dressed in their Sunday best. The resolute determination his parents displayed in the face of poverty would fuel Morrison's unyielding drive for success for the rest of his life.

While growing up in Glendale, Marion Morrison earned a moniker that would transcend his lifetime. The young man's companionship with the family dog, an Airedale named Duke, led to the two being called "Big Duke" and "Little Duke." From that declaration forward, he would be affectionately known as Duke to all who knew him. It was just one more legacy from his childhood that would serve him well throughout his life, along with his work ethic, his humility and his compassion for those who were down on their luck—values every American can admire.

John Wayne poses for a picture with his younger brother Robert, his parents and the family dog. As an adult, Robert worked behind the scenes on several of Duke's films, including *McLintock!* (1963).

School Days

After his family made the move to Glendale, California, Duke began attending Glendale High School as part of the 1925 graduating class. Immediately, the future Western star threw himself into a variety of extracurricular activities and became the ultimate overachiever. The 170-pound teenager joined the football team as a guard and, in addition to battling it out on the field, Duke's byline "M.M.M." graced the sports section of the school newspaper, *The Explosion*. The young man even had time to act in two school plays, *Dulcy* and *The First Lady of the Land*, which introduced him to the thrill and joy of being an actor.

Opposite page: A young Marion Morrison in a Glendale High School yearbook photo from 1924; a copy of the 1924 edition of Glendale High School's yearbook. This page: As a young man, Duke had good looks to spare. He put his classically handsome features to use during a variety show put on by his high school in Glendale, modeling the latest female fashions of the day in a humorous sketch.

Guests watch fencers spar a round during a 1920s party. F. Scott Fitzgerald's *The Great Gatsby*, which depicted the lavish parties of the '20s, was published in 1925.

★ 1925–1930 ★
ON THE RISE

 S THE 1920s took shape as a time of unprecedented prosperity for the U.S. after its victory in World War I, the nation, still an adolescent on the world stage, forged a position for itself through sheer will. At the same time John Wayne, who was studying at the University of Southern California, was beginning to do the same. After proving himself in the classroom and on the gridiron at Glendale High, the USC Trojans offered Duke a football scholarship under legendary coach Howard Jones, one of the first of the game's innovators to embrace the forward pass. It seemed, for a while, that nothing could go wrong, but when it did both John Wayne and the U.S. were able, throughout the '20s, to reach ever upward no matter what. Sidelined by injury and forced to quit the football team, Duke didn't wallow. Instead, he established himself in a new niche in the motion picture industry. Likewise, when America's prosperity seemed threatened by tragedy, including the death of the 1920s first elected president, Warren Harding, the country was determined to meet adversity with success.

The 1920s stand out in the country's history for a variety of reasons—the rise of a national popular culture, the increasing independence of women and the birth of modern consumerism—but all of these remarkable changes were made possible by the decade's booming economy. Between the years of 1920 and 1929, the United States economy grew by an estimated 59 percent, a boom fueled by the advent (and success) of entirely new industries such as automobiles and luxury home goods.

Events abroad also gave the American economy a tremendous lift. World War I had either completely devastated most of the world's other developed economies or placed upon them a tremendous financial strain. But the relatively late arrival by the U.S. to the war, plus its distance from the destruction of the frontlines, meant the industrial might of the country was unscathed. In addition, the U.S. had loaned the Allied nations large sums of money and supplies, and after the Treaty of Versailles was signed in 1919 (a project spearheaded by the world leaders known as The Big Four, pictured below), these nations owed America about $10 billion. In short, the country was in an extremely advantageous financial position following WWI.

This influx of money wasn't cause for celebration for only the Treasury Department—America's middle class suddenly found itself empowered economically as wages rose throughout the decade. From 1921 to 1924 alone, employees' net income increased by 18 percent, and throughout the entire decade unemployment never rose above 4 percent, meaning more people were earning money than ever before.

The Roaring '20s also marked a turning point in America's culture, and young working women, who had just earned the right to vote with the ratification of the 19th Amendment in 1920, were experiencing a revolution of their own. And despite Prohibition laws, which were in place from 1920 until 1933, an influx of money and a newfound sense of independence meant social drinking, in jazz clubs and speakeasies, was perhaps more popular than ever during this decade.

The explosion in new luxury goods able to cut down the time Americans spent doing household chores also meant, for many, an unprecedented amount of free time to pursue leisure activities. Radio became the nation's first truly mass-produced and mass-consumed media, offering a common slate of music and programs enjoyed by Americans from Boston to Burbank. Airwaves from hundreds of stations streamed into more than 12 million homes by the end of the 1920s, and programs such as *The Grand Ole Opry*, *Mystery House* and others became cultural touchstones helping unify the country. This in turn strengthened the growing bond between Americans and their favorite games. Listening to baseball and football on the radio was the beginning of modern sports culture as we know it.

Americans also began a love affair with another form of popular entertainment—the

From top: A family enjoys a night of entertainment from their radio, 1930s. The decade prior saw the rise of consumer luxury goods in America that made the scene pictured possible; a painting of flappers, 1923.

movies. By 1930, 65 percent of the population attended the movies once a week. Larger-than-life stories about romance, warfare and the drama of everyday life didn't just entertain audiences—they influenced what Americans expected from their own lives. "The height of my desire was to be of an age where fine clothes, parties, an ardent lover would not be out of place," a 20-year-old college coed reported as part of a 1933 study on how movies affected American society, conducted by University of Chicago sociologist Herbert Blumer. "I longed to be a society belle, and my ambitions seemed to be realized when I was able to see the objects of my fancy on the screen. Of course, I believed that life was exactly as it was painted and that at the age when I would be able to go out, life would be a sort of bed of roses." Movie stars also helped popularize the image of the flapper, whose distinctive wardrobe was only matched by her brazen frankness regarding matters of independence and sex. The flapper quickly became an icon for the exuberant, devil-may-care nature of the decade that treated life as a never-ending

party—the perfect mascot for an era defined by its optimism. America was on the rise, and in the eyes of her citizens, it seemed nothing could slow her down.

College Man

An accomplished competitor on the gridiron during his high school days, Duke parlayed his athleticism into a football scholarship at USC, where he hoped to acquire the education necessary to build his bright future. The scholarship covered the full cost of tuition ($280 a year) and a single meal a day with the team, provided you were an active player. The free lunch also only applied five days a week, which meant that Duke had to come up with the funds to fill his belly when not with the team. Fortunately, few undergrads before and since have possessed the self-reliance and independent spirit of Duke, and the young man managed to get by on odd jobs around campus, such as serving food at sorority houses. Duke's football career at USC came to an end after injuring his shoulder in a body surfing accident, but his time as a Trojan led him to Hollywood—and eventually stardom.

From left: John Wayne (back row, second from right) with Ann Dvorak and Pat O'Brien (second from left) among other friends; two images of Duke in his football gear as a Trojan for USC. Duke's experience helped him bring authenticity to roles in football films, such as *Brown of Harvard* (1926).

John Ford (seated wearing a hat) on the set of *Men Without Women* (1930). The movie had featured John Wayne in a bit part as a radio operator.

Leaving Football, Finding a Coach

Even before his on-screen presence made him the most beloved Western star of all time, his sheer physicality was the first characteristic one was likely to notice about young Marion Morrison. Tall and confident, Duke was also a rare athlete in the early 1920s, when a football-crazed nation valued his 6'4", 225-pound frame enough to place the standout under the tutelage of Howard Jones, founder of the USC Trojan football dynasty and one of the first true innovators of the game.

During his time on both the Glendale High and USC football teams, Duke called upon a passion for hard work learned in his youth and realized his first modicum of success in one of the most testing physical environments possible—the nearly padless and bone-crushing violence of leather helmet football. And it would be the same skills he learned on the gridiron, both physical and ethical, that would give young Morrison a break in show business.

AS SOON AS FORD WAS READY TO TAKE THE HIT, DUKE SWEPT THE DIRECTOR'S LEGS OUT FROM UNDER HIM.

Director John Ford was a man who could appreciate Duke Morrison's unique kind of strength and presence, being a former gridiron man himself and one of the most hardscrabble Americans in this great nation's history. So when the two crossed paths on the set of the auteur's *Mother Machree*, it came as no surprise that their meeting was portentous for the history of strong, captivating leading men in cinema. Working various odd jobs for the studio—on this particular day he was herding geese—Duke was trying to make ends meet after being sidelined from USC's football team (and therefore, his scholarship) by his bodysurfing injury.

When Ford noticed Duke—a USC championship-caliber tackle awkwardly herding geese—the veteran director and noted prankster couldn't resist having some fun with the confident young football player. Calling Duke over to him, Ford struck up a conversation about football, eventually goading the younger man into taking his three-point stance

right there on set. When Duke obliged, Ford wasted little time in deftly kicking his limbs out from under him.

Sprawled out on the floor and subject to the laughs of those on set, Duke calmly got up as Ford challenged him again. "You're not much of a guard," the older man is supposed to have said before commenting that Duke couldn't knock him down if he tried. Duke, with revenge on his mind, obliged. As soon as Ford was ready to take the hit, Duke swept the director's legs out from under him, leaving Ford sprawled on the ground in the same place Duke had been just moments earlier.

If Duke was ever nervous about whether this stunt might cost him a job, those anxieties were quickly eased when Ford rose from the ground but remained doubled over in laughter. A director-actor friendship the likes of which cinema sees perhaps once a generation was born. It was also one of the art form's most fruitful, though it was slow to begin. Beyond the small roles Ford provided Duke in the late 1920s, the actor didn't appear in any significant way in Ford's films until 1939's *Stagecoach*.

During their decades-long relationship, Duke would call Ford "Pop" or "Coach," both names signifying the deep respect Duke Morrison had for the man who helped him become John Wayne. When "Coach" finally succumbed after a lifetime of challenging death at every opportunity, John Wayne, weakened from his own battle with cancer, took out a full page ad in *Variety* thanking the old stalwart for providing him with "a wonderful and eventful life."

John Wayne on the set of *The Black Watch* (1929), an early John Ford movie. The film was Ford's first that featured sound.

Unemployed men wait in line outside a Chicago soup kitchen opened by notorious criminal Al Capone, 1931. Though many wrote the effort off as a publicity stunt to improve his image, a 1931 *Chicago Tribune* headline stated Capone's soup kitchen had served 120,000 meals.

★ 1930–1939 ★
TOUGH TIMES, TOUGHER PEOPLE

WHEN THE COUNTRY crashed after the decade-long revelry of the 1920s, it crashed hard. Just as it seemed John Wayne might be making his way onto the A-list, the Great Depression changed just about every American's idea of what the 1930s would be like. There was a lot of scraping and surviving ahead, for both the country and Duke, as he worked his way back through B-pictures after the relative failure of his first leading role in the big budget film, *The Big Trail* (1930), which was released shortly after the crash.

As Duke and the rest of the country's hard-working citizens buckled down for what would soon be called the Devil's Decade, they knew and took to heart the fact that America has always considered itself a land of plenty. Lying at the core of the American dream is the implicit bargain that if you work hard enough (and maybe catch a few breaks), you'll find your reward of material comfort. It's a deal that has been honored unevenly since our independence, a reflection of the imperfections that come with any organization of fallible human beings, but it's worked enough to inspire generations of dreamers—both at home and abroad—to believe they can find their best futures in the

A New York man attempts to sell his car for $100 after losing everything on Black Thursday. In 2017, that would be an asking price of approximately $1,400.

United States. The sense of optimism buoying the American experience suffered a crushing blow during the 1930s, a decade marred by deprivation, destitution and disgrace. The Great Depression is known as the economic crisis beginning at the tail end of 1929 and lasted roughly until Hitler plunged the planet into World War II. It didn't just empty bank accounts and upend lives—it challenged the very notion that life in America would always be one free from wants, that tomorrow would always be brighter than today.

When the icy cold water of financial reality woke the country from its dream of a perpetually rising stock market, many discovered they had lost nearly everything. And the worst was yet to come. With the stock market in shambles, businesses circled the wagons and ceased placing large orders for goods and products, convinced consumers wouldn't continue spending money on refrigerators, toaster ovens and the like as they had during the Roaring '20s. This realization came far too late, as demand had already begun slowing down in the summer before the stock market crash, but the events of late October catalyzed the flaws inherent in the economy with a volatility that crippled the nation. With everyone from the titans of industry in their corner offices to the owners of mom and pop shops on Main Street cutting back on their expenses, many workers suddenly found their services were no longer needed, as industrial production fell 47 percent from 1929 to 1933.

The Depression didn't quash the growth of the film industry, however. If anything, the hard times experienced across the country furthered the need for inexpensive forms of escape, and with the addition of sound to motion pictures (beginning in 1927, with *The Jazz Singer*), "talkies" were becoming the talk of the town, and not just in the theaters. Local merchants in communities across the country would occasionally pool their resources to screen free films on the sides of their buildings in an effort to attract penny-pinching consumers to the town shopping district. Hollywood studios churned out B-pictures with shoestring budgets; escapist stories of sword fights and derring-do; of cowboys and castles and comebacks. *My Man Godfrey* (1936), one of the most beloved pictures from this period, stars Carole Lombard as a wealthy socialite who selects Godfrey (William Powell), a down-on-his-luck banker, to be her butler. This story of a man who lost it all but

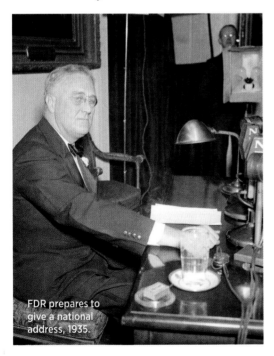

FDR prepares to give a national address, 1935.

found redemption is just one example of how Hollywood's creations helped to lift the spirits of our nation during this dark time.

But perhaps no one had more impact on the national psyche during the Great Depression than our 32nd president. The suffering of huge swaths of the American electorate helped hand president Herbert Hoover a crushing defeat from Democrat Franklin Delano Roosevelt in the 1932 presidential election. FDR aggressively worked with Congress to push through the New Deal, a series of programs and projects meant to provide relief to the country. Acronyms such as the CCC (Civilian Conservation Corps) the WPA (Works Progress Administration) and the TVA (Tennessee Valley Authority) helped reshape the American landscape (sometimes literally, as public works projects such as the Hoover Dam were the result of Roosevelt's New Deal).

While these programs may have restored some faith in the government's ability to tackle the economic crisis, they certainly didn't end the Depression. As with its origins, the conclusion of the Depression was caused by myriad factors that economists still argue over today. One popular theory gives credit to the industrial needs of World War II as putting America back on the path to prosperity, though others point to the fact that the country's GDP had largely recovered by 1939—evidence that the nation would have soon been back on its feet without a new world war. No matter what caused the end of the Depression, Americans were grateful for the conclusion of their economic nightmare, despite an even greater threat to their way of life encroaching from abroad. It would be the fight against this threat, fascism, that would ultimately bring the U.S. to full recovery thanks to the production required to quash the menace.

From left: John Wayne and Marguerite Churchill in *The Big Trail* (1930); two painted lobby cards depicting Duke and actor Tully Marshall in the film. Marshall and John Wayne would later appear together in one of Duke's lesser-known films, *California Straight Ahead!* (1937).

The Big Trail

John Wayne's first lead role in a movie was nearly his last. In fact, it was the first time Marion Morrison used the name John Wayne, a moniker given to him by the studio and director Raoul Walsh because they felt his given name wasn't manly enough for the theater marquee. Plucked from obscurity to star in *The Big Trail* (1930), Duke found himself anchoring a tale of settlers striking out for a new life, a yarn as American as apple pie. But the beginning of the Great Depression cast a gloom over the marquee lights of *The Big Trail*, dooming it to box office disappointment and transforming John Wayne's big break into a spectacular case of bad timing. Examining the film with the distance of a few decades, today's audiences can clearly see *The Big Trail* for what it is—a singularly ambitious, American piece of storytelling made all the more compelling because of the failure inflicted upon it by forces outside its control.

How Duke ended up in the leading role of an epic, ambitious Hollywood production commanding a budget of about $2 million (worth about $29 million in today's money) when the 23-year-old only had a smattering of small roles on his résumé remains a point of contention. According to documentarian Richard Schickel (and friend of the film's director Raoul Walsh), Walsh spotted Duke's star potential as the young man was lugging equipment around on the set of Fox Film.

"Walsh says he saw Wayne carrying a chair or something in the props department," Schickel told *True West* magazine in 2008. "And, as he tells the story, he went over to

[Duke] and chatted with him and asked if he wanted to be in a picture. And they did a test—I don't think it was a talking test—it was a kind of in-costume, silent test. And they put him in a nice pair of buckskins, which he wore in the picture, and asked, 'How'd you like to be an actor?' And he said, 'I'd like to do that.'"

The Big Trail was one of the rare instances (maybe the only one) where John Wayne was dwarfed by the grandeur of the film in which he starred. The brainchild of Walsh, a director who worked on films such as *The Thief of Bagdad* (1924), *The Big Trail* aimed to launch the Western into a new strata of artistry.

To tell the story of a wagon train making the arduous trek on the Oregon Trail during the West's frontier days, Walsh demanded extensive outdoor shoots featuring 20,000 extras, almost 200 covered wagons and thousands of cattle and horses. Adding to the complexity of the undertaking was the use of 70mm cameras to shoot footage, allowing cinematographer Arthur Edeson to capture scenes of breathtaking scope at the cost of constant care and upkeep of the lenses needed for such a feat—no easy task, when shooting in harsh environments such as Yuma, Arizona, and Jackson Hole, Wyoming.

"It became a hard and fast rule that the cameras must be cleaned thoroughly every night, not only with brushes but with compressed air streams," wrote Edeson in the September 1930 issue of *American Cinematographer*. Despite the daunting challenges confronting Walsh and his team,

the movie's epic scope and breathtaking spectacle have awed audiences for generations. "The oddly meditative quality of Walsh's long takes, the curious lack of a dominant narrative tension controlling the film's space and the oddly disjunct tableau-to-tableau editing combine to make a statement quite different from that of the typical Hollywood film," wrote critic Fred Camper in 1988 for a retrospective review in the *Chicago Reader*. "Walsh has given us a rare vision of nature, one that is not man-centered; his film is permeated with a powerful, mysterious sense of an always-looming, weighty, abstracted empty space."

As alluded to in Camper's review (and countless others), the performances in *The Big Trail* often feel dwarfed by the film's more expansive elements. Tyrone Power Sr., who plays the villainous trapper Red Flack, looks particularly lost. A star of the silent era whose boyish good looks made him a

Duke (second from right) takes aim in a scene from the film.

John Wayne and a Native American from the Crow tribe share a scene in the movie. *The Big Trail* was released in 1930, a mere 40 years after The Massacre at Wounded Knee. The conflict was considered the last major battle between the United States and various Native American tribes.

favorite of directors, Power had swollen into a burly mass of a man struggling with the relatively recent addition of sound to film. "Tyrone Power was just awful in that picture—disastrous performance—stagy, over the top," Schickel says. Critics gave John Wayne a more generous appraisal, with a 1930 *New York Times* review claiming, "His performance is pleasingly natural and even if he is somewhat fortunate in settling matters in a closing scene with the ignominious Red Flack and his cohort, Lopez, one feels that he is entitled to this stroke of luck." Still, as that same review would note, the story and acting of the film played a definite second-fiddle to *The Big Trail*'s extravagance.

The movie made a huge impact at the box office—though not in the way anyone involved had hoped. Few movie theaters in the country possessed the equipment needed to show the film in all of its 70mm glory, and audiences still in shock from the 1929 stock market crash weren't clamoring to spend their money at the movies. The film made only around $900,000 in the domestic market, drowning John Wayne's would-be stardom in a sea of red ink. The world would have to wait another decade before Duke took his rightful place among Hollywood's headliners, but today's fans of John Wayne can appreciate *The Big Trail* as a noble failure that set a young man on the path to becoming a Western icon.

Climbing the Ladder

The true cost of the Great Depression can't be measured in lost wages or missing stock dividends, but in the depressing number of dreams deferred by everyday Americans. Like others across the country, John Wayne spent the time period trying to make ends meet, and he was lucky (and talented) enough to be able to do so in his chosen profession. Duke put in more than his fair share of time cutting his teeth on-screen in sporadic small roles and less-than-stellar pictures. These gigs, which were steady and numerous for several years, would begin to illuminate the star quality John Wayne eventually displayed in full force.

Shunned from upper echelons of Hollywood thanks to the dismal performance of *The Big Trail* (1930), Duke focused on low-budget serials and rapidly filmed B-Westerns, including the darkly humorous *Haunted Gold* in 1932 and 1934's *The Lucky Texan*, a tale of two men who find gold and fend off crooks interested in taking it from them.

Amid the serials and B-Westerns, John Wayne's résumé also included roles that would strike modern audiences as wildly uncharacteristic of the tough-as-nails American icon. While filmgoers watching *Stagecoach* (1939) could hardly tear their

Duke woos a señorita in a scene from *The Man from Monterey* (1933).

John Wayne shows he is all business in *Idol of the Crowds* (1937). The movie was one of the eight B-movies Duke made for Universal Pictures between 1936 and 1937.

John Wayne with Lois Moran in *Words and Music* (1929). The musical also included a bit role for Ward Bond, friend and frequent costar of Duke's throughout the icon's career.

eyes from Duke's Ringo Kid, John Wayne's sole contribution to the 1931 mystery *The Deceiver* was as a stand-in corpse. And while the actor's later characters would cause plenty of lonely frontier women to swoon in delight, he played a true cad in 1933's *His Private Secretary*, a romantic comedy showcasing Duke's powers of seduction. In 1937, John Wayne swapped his pistol and boots for a hockey stick and skates in

the sports drama *Idol of the Crowds*. His performance required more skill than most of his work had up to that point, given that the California-raised Duke had to convincingly portray a guy who felt at home on the ice. Even though the actor had a tough time standing on his skates, he pulled it off—a testament to the work ethic and never-quit attitude that served him well throughout his career.

From left: Evalyn Knapp, John Wayne and Natalie Kingston in a scene from *His Private Secretary* (1933).

Poster Boy

Never one to shy away from hard work, Duke made more than 60 B-movies during the 1930s. He got plenty of practice playing cowboy, though he also got to try his hand at acting in dramas and romance films. Though it must have been disappointing to work on Poverty Row after *The Big Trail* was supposed to have launched him into stardom, John Wayne never complained. He knew the money he earned at the time (his 1932 film *Ride Him, Cowboy* earned the actor $850, for instance) was more than many could call their own.

Arizona
1931

Girls Demand Excitement *1931*

The Range Feud
1931

Three Girls Lost
1931

The Big Stampede
1932

The Shadow of the Eagle *1932*

That's My Boy
1932

Two-Fisted Law
1932

His Private Secretary
1933

**Riders of
Destiny** *1933*

**Somewhere in
Sonora** *1933*

Blue Steel
1934

**The Man From
Utah** *1934*

**Randy Rides
Alone** *1934*

The Star Packer
1934

The Trail Beyond
1934

**West of the
Divide** *1934*

The Dawn Rider
1935

The Desert Trail
1935

The New Frontier
1935

Westward Ho
1935

Conflict
1936

The Lonely Trail
1936

The Oregon Trail
1936

The Sea Spoilers
1936

Adventure's End
1937

**California Straight
Ahead!** *1937*

I Cover the War!
1937

Pals of the Saddle
1938

John Wayne and his wife Josephine (right of Duke) with Loretta Young and William Powell at the Beverly Hills Brown Derby. Young and Duke starred together in *Three Girls Lost* in 1931, one of the films Duke worked on during the Great Depression.

The Loves of His Life

A big man with a big heart, Duke was lucky enough to find love three times during his life. After a courtship that lasted several years, he married Josephine Saenz, the daughter of a Panamanian diplomat, in 1933. The young couple enjoyed soaking up the California sunshine during the day and relaxing with friends well into the evening. They had four children together (Toni, Michael, Patrick and Melinda), but the pressure of John Wayne's burgeoning film career led the pair to realize they wanted different things from life. They agreed to an amicable separation in 1945.

Clockwise from left: Duke and Josephine with their eldest child, Michael; John Wayne and his new bride Josephine on their wedding day, June 24, 1933, with bridesmaid Loretta Young. Young's family hosted the nuptials at their Bel Air home; John Wayne sitting on a chair at his Hollywood home and reading a *Prince Valiant* comic with his children (from left) Patrick, Melinda, Toni and Michael.

Duke pulls Michael, Patrick, Toni and Melinda around the Republic Studios lot. Republic became one of the most important studios in Duke's career, and the actor became its biggest star after 1939's *Stagecoach*.

Stagecoach

After honing his skills and talents for almost a decade during the Great Depression, John Wayne finally received the opportunity he had been working toward when he was cast as the Ringo Kid in *Stagecoach* (1939). And he didn't squander it. When audiences first saw Duke in his breakout film, they witnessed John Wayne finally fufilling his cinematic potential. The scene begins with the crack of a rifle shot, and (what is now) a familiar voice blending stern authority with youthful exuberance shouting, "Hold it!" The camera cuts to John Wayne as the Ringo Kid, in the prime of his life, ready to write his own legend. He then expertly twirls his Winchester rifle in a gesture that broadcasts the absolute confidence of both character and actor before the camera zooms in on Duke, briefly losing focus before crystallizing with total clarity on a face that would soon become as associated with America as the bald eagle, apple pie and Old Glory. It's a scene that captures the appeal of Duke as a movie star like never before, and one that still remains a go-to example of the actor's unique charisma.

It was an introduction that almost never came to pass. According to most accounts (including Duke's own unpublished biography), director and mentor John Ford casually asked Duke in 1938 whom he should cast as the Ringo Kid for the upcoming film. John Wayne, with typical humility and honesty, suggested actor Lloyd Nolan (a solid performer also known for starring in B-movie Westerns). "Hell, Duke, can't you play it?" Ford countered, according to Michael Goldman's book *The Genuine Article*. After nine years of languishing in the purgatory of B-movies, John Wayne found himself with the opportunity to turn back the clock and have another shot at A-list stardom—all he had to do was not screw it up.

Duke joined a cast filled with actors trusted by Ford to take his often-demanding direction and deliver performances up to his high standards. This included Claire Trevor as Dallas, the lady of ill repute with a 24-carat heart; Thomas Mitchell as the alcohol-soaked Doc Boone; the put-upon lawman Marshal Curley Wilcox (George Bancroft); the Southern dandy gambler Hatfield (John Carradine); and more. None of these characters broke the mold in terms of originality when looked at on paper—Western writers had been using these well-worn archetypes since the advent of the genre. But screenwriter Dudley Nichols, Ford and the actors were able to present these tropes at their best to make them seem fresh and exciting for the audience. Even today, the interplay between the various characters on their journey via

John Wayne and
Claire Trevor in
a scene from
Stagecoach (1939).

stagecoach to the town of Lordsburg provides most of the excitement, the arguments and (in the case of the Ringo Kid and Dallas) romance, cementing the film as a compelling classic.

Together, all of these elements coalesced into one of the most celebrated movies in Duke's oeuvre. "It's absorbing drama without the general theatrics usual to picturizations of the early West," read the *Variety* review at the time of *Stagecoach*'s release. *The New York Times* acknowledged that the film didn't blaze any new trails with its narrative or characters, while

also assuring readers it didn't matter. "Foreknowledge doesn't cheat Mr. Ford of his thrills," the review reads. "His attitude, if it spoke its mind, would be: 'All right, you know what's coming, but have you ever seen it done like this?' And once you've swallowed your heart again, you'll have to say: 'No, sir! Not like this!'" For John Wayne, the film was a complete game changer. Having proved himself more than capable of commanding a compelling big-screen performance, Duke would leave the B-movies behind him. From then on, he was America's leading man.

★ PAGES FROM A PRESS BOOK released by United Artists (which distributed *Stagecoach* for Walter Wanger Productions) to help promote the Western. Materials found in the book include small biographies of the film's principal actors, commentary on Claire Trevor's wardrobe and a summary of the movie's premise. ★

Smoke billows from the USS *Yorktown* during the Battle of Midway, 1942. The battle took place six months after the attacks on Pearl Harbor.

★1939–1949★
WORLD AT WAR

THOUGH WORLD WAR II began in 1939 with Adolf Hitler's invasion of Poland, the United States avoided direct involvement in the conflict until December 7, 1941, when Japan launched a military strike against American naval fleets off the coast of Hawaii at Pearl Harbor. One day later, the United States and Britain declared war on Japan. Three days after that, Italy and Germany declared war on the U.S.

Japan's bombing of Pearl Harbor did more than force America's hand in going to war—it set off a nationwide panic in its citizens, who feared a similar attack could be coming to the mainland, especially along the Pacific coast. Though this feeling of alarm resulted in some regrettable decisions (such as the internment of Japanese Americans), it also encouraged Americans of all stripes to figuratively—and sometimes literally—pull on their boots and get to work. Virtually every man, woman and child felt emboldened to help the war effort and protect their country in whatever ways they could. As John Wayne said of American spirit, "It's an outlook, an attitude." And during World War II, it was an attitude Americans

A woman operates a lathe at the Consolidated Aircraft Corportation in Texas, 1942. Five million women entered America's workforce between 1940 and 1945.

embraced wholeheartedly, whether they were part of the 2 million who were inducted into the military or one of the millions more who supported their country on the home front.

For as long as America was at war, virtually every American was subject to rations, for everything from food to gas, tires, clothing and fuel oil. To help boost morale and remind citizens their sacrifice was valued, the United States Office of War Information created now-iconic posters reminding citizens to "Do with less—so they'll have enough!"

Meanwhile, as Americans struggled to adapt to the new realities of war, suspicion began to overtake us. Not only did the U.S. place its citizens of Japanese ancestry in internment camps throughout the duration of the war, 1945 also marked the beginning of this suspicious tendency manifesting in a new way that would define the next decade: fear of communism. Though we counted Stalin as an ally during the war, Americans took

to heart Winston Churchill's warning about Russia being a riddle wrapped in mystery and enigma, and by the time the war died down communists were imagined to be hiding in every industry.

Each of these industries were also cast into upheaval throughout the war and its aftermath. At a time when there was an endless demand for airplanes, warships, rifles and tanks, the very men who usually worked in factories to build those machines had been sent off to war. Men plied every trade under the sun in the service of the American military—John Ford, for example, was hit with shrapnel while filming for the Navy during the Battle of Midway (his 1942 film of the same name would win an Academy Award for Best Documentary) and John Wayne—a bona fide star following the success of *Stagecoach*—and many others were active in entertaining troops through the newly founded USO. As a result, women picked up the slack. Encouraged by the famous Rosie the Riveter campaign, women entered many fields that had previously been exclusively available to men, working as welders, electricians and riveters.

In May 1942, Congress launched the Women's Auxiliary Army Corps, which would later become the Women's Army Corps. Within three years, more than 100,000 women were WACs, serving in noncombatant stateside jobs. The Navy followed suit, recruiting members for Women Accepted for Volunteer Emergency Service (WAVES). By the fall, women were also joining the Marine Corps, serving in a wide variety of positions so more men would be available for combat roles.

When V-J Day finally brought World War II to a close in August 1945, the ecstatic revelry that had greeted GIs as they liberated villages and cities across Europe finally made its way back home. America's sons—and thousands of daughters—were on their way home, and the U.S. was ready to celebrate.

Americans flocked to theaters to see films like *The Best Years of Our Lives*, which dealt with the emotional aftermath of war, and the patriotic cinema of the war years continued as Hollywood allowed itself to revel in victory. John Wayne, increasingly in demand as a leading man, made two of his most beloved patriotic pictures, *Back to Bataan* and *They Were Expendable*, in 1945. By 1949, the Hollywood formula for postwar patriotism was so locked-in, it was ready to produce its masterpiece with John Wayne's Oscar-nominated role in *Sands of Iwo Jima*.

Even before Duke was paying his respects to American GIs on-screen, Washington, D.C. was cooking up a bigger tribute. The first draft of the GI Bill was proposed in January 1944, approved by Congress six months later and signed into law on June 22, 1944, more than a year before the Allies claimed victory.

The GI Bill granted benefits to all veterans of WWII, regardless of income or gender. By 1956, benefits (including guaranteed loans, unemployment benefits, medical care and college tuition) had been extended to almost 10 million vets.

The end of the war also launched the baby boom: In 1946, more babies were born in the United States than ever before. There were 3.4 million births in 1946, a full 20 percent more than the previous year. This phenomenon was more than a one-off burst of exuberance celebrating the conclusion of the war: The number of births continued to rise, with 3.8 million babies born in 1947, 3.9 million in 1952 and more than 4 million births every year between 1954 and 1964, when the boom finally started to recede. By that point, "baby boomers" accounted for almost 40 percent of the U.S. population.

New York City celebrates V-J Day, 1945. Japan's formal surrender took place aboard the USS *Missouri* in Tokyo Bay.

Tour of Duty

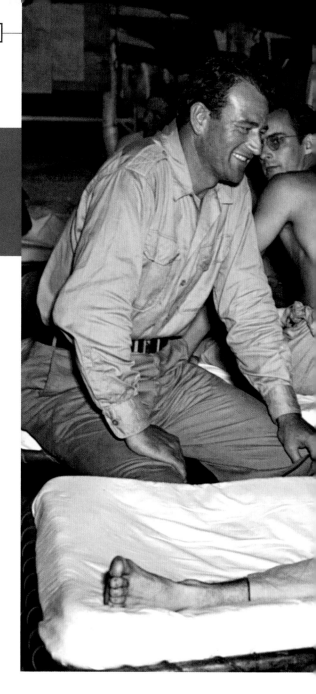

Just after Christmas of 1943, John Wayne left the comfort of his California home for the war-torn South Pacific, where he would spend the next three months touring with the USO. From bases in Brisbane, Australia, to hospitals in New Britain, Duke performed for the American troops and used all of his talents to raise spirits and boost morale. Whenever he felt tired, cold or hungry, all he had to do was look out at the thousands of men who'd had it far worse for far longer, and his passionate patriotism energized him to finish the show.

Duke lived by the mantra "talk low, talk slow and don't say too much," but he made an exception for the men and women in uniform looking for a little laughter in the middle of a war zone. The actor would close shows with renditions of call-and-response classics such as "Minnie the Moocher," and the laconic, Western idol busting into rapid-fire scat brought the house down every time. "They enjoy seeing us [celebrities] because it reminds them of home," he wrote to his daughter, Toni, while touring. As happy as Duke was to help put on some entertainment for the troops, chewing the fat over a couple drinks was more the man's style. In combat zones, he was just like everyone else—swapping stories and swatting flies in the 100-degree jungles of the South Pacific, praying his

base wouldn't be bombed. He refused special treatment and would eat, drink and sleep just like the servicemen.

While in the South Pacific, John Wayne was also tasked with collecting information for the OSS, an organization comparable to the modern day CIA. Duke was to report back his impressions of the soldiers and officers serving abroad, particularly

Gen. Douglas MacArthur. But much to the actor's disappointment, he never met MacArthur, and he returned stateside empty-handed.

Although his tour ended, Duke continued to fight for the troops fighting for him. After arriving home, he held a press conference to share his experiences and rally both moral and material support for the men abroad. "What the guys down there need are letters and cigars, more snapshots, phonograph needles and radios," Duke said at a press conference after his USO tour. Even though John Wayne was thousands of miles from the front, the memories of soldiers enjoying a brief respite from the hell of combat still remained in his heart.

The Fighting Seabees

During the years of World War II, John Wayne lent his considerable talents to helping out on the home front in any way he could. Sometimes this would mean showing up at the Hollywood Canteen in Los Angeles to serve Thanksgiving turkey to hungry servicemen, or to tour the country urging his fellow citizens to buy war bonds. But his biggest impact was felt at the cinema, where the actor helped keep morale high with movies lionizing the deeds of America's soldiers. After the attack on Pearl Harbor, Americans expected more from Hollywood than mere entertainment—audiences craved uplifting stories to help ease the doubt and fear they felt as the world plunged into violent chaos. Fortunately, they had John Wayne waiting in the wings, the very model of American strength, dignity and hope for a better future.

Duke starred in his first war movie in 1942's *Flying Tigers*, but his second film to fully focus on the conflict was

Clockwise from left: A poster for the film; John Wayne and J. M. Kerrigan in a scene from *The Fighting Seabees* (1944). Kerrigan had shared the screen with Duke before in *The Long Voyage Home* (1940).

The Fighting Seabees. The movie strives to accomplish more than just provide a few scenes of American soldiers routing Japanese troops—it tells the story of a group of skilled but stubborn civilians who learn a painful lesson about the necessity of militarization and discipline, something millions of Americans could relate to by the time of the film's 1944 release. Duke plays Wedge Donovan, the head of a construction crew responsible for

helping the Navy construct airstrips, bases and anything else the military needed to occupy and fortify the Pacific islands. The beginning of the film sees Donovan clashing with Lt. Cmdr. Robert Yarrow (Dennis O'Keefe) over the Navy's refusal to arm his construction crew, who are unable to defend themselves against attacks by the Japanese. Yarrow and Donovan quickly agree on the unsustainability of the status quo, but differ on how to solve

From left: Duke in *The Fighting Seabees*; real-life Seabees gather around actress Susan Hayward, whom they crowned the first Seabee Queen in 1943. The Seabee Queen presided over the festivities surrounding the Seabee Ball until the position was discontinued in 1992.

the strong arms of Donovan. After a Japanese attack leaves much of Donovan's crew (included Constance) wounded, the hot-headed construction boss realizes the error of his ways and supports Yarrow's efforts to form a construction battalion, called the Seabees. Now strictly by the book, Donovan leads the battalion with model discipline and valor, going so far as to sacrifice himself during another battle against the Japanese in order to secure victory for the Navy.

Republic Pictures poured $1.5 million into the production of *The Fighting Seabees*, making the patriotic film the biggest one yet for a movie studio still focused mainly on B-movies and which emphasized cost-cutting measures. Though he had yet to achieve the cultural dominance he would enjoy during the 1950s and beyond, John Wayne was clearly Republic's biggest attraction, and the studio kept finding ways to satisfy his larger-than-life ambitions. Scenes for

the problem—Yarrow wants to form a battalion of construction workers under the auspices of the Navy, while Donovan balks at the length of time it would take for his men to complete training. Complicating matters between the two men is a shared affection for journalist Constance Chesley (Susan Hayward), who can't decide for much of the movie whether she should remain true to her beau Yarrow or follow her passion into

From top: A pith helmet worn by Duke in the movie from the John Wayne Archive; (from left) William Frawley, J. M. Kerrigan, Susan Hayward, John Wayne and Grant Withers in a scene from the film. Frawley later found fame as Fred Mertz in the television series *I Love Lucy*; Dennis O'Keefe, Susan Hayward and John Wayne in a scene from the movie.

the movie were filmed at Port Hueneme, located in Southern California and still the home port for the Seabees today, as well as Iverson Movie Ranch, a 30-acre outdoor expanse that provided scenery for thousands of films, from the silent era all the way through 1997. Much of *The Fighting Seabees* production budget went into transforming the Southern California landscape into an approximation of the hellscape of the Pacific Islands during war, complete with fake palm trees and plenty of pyrotechnics to simulate the explosive mortar attacks and air raids of the Japanese.

But for audiences both at the time of the film's release and today, the most important takeaway of *The Fighting Seabees* isn't its scenes of warfare, but the emotional honesty of the message the movie gets across. Perhaps appropriate for a movie made during wartime, *The Fighting Seabees* doesn't shy from showing the tragic aftermath of battle, even one ending in victory for the good guys. And Donovan's slow realization that his selfishness has no place in the fight for freedom is one of the most poignant performances in John Wayne's career. World War II may have ended more than seven decades ago, but that lesson remains just as vital today as in years past.

John Wayne and Susan Hayward in *The Fighting Seabees*. Hayward would star with Duke again in *The Conqueror* (1956).

Duke in one of *Sands of Iwo Jima*'s thrilling battle scenes. In addition to featuring stunning pyrotechnics and one of the most realistic sets to date, the movie weaved in archival newsreel footage of battles to increase the feeling of authenticity for audiences. Right: A poster for *Sands of Iwo Jima*.

Sands of Iwo Jima

THE MARINES' GREATEST HOUR

SANDS OF IWO JIMA

JOHN WAYNE

JOHN AGAR · ADELE MARA · FORREST TUCKER

WALLY CASSELL·JAMES BROWN·RICHARD WEBB · ARTHUR FRANZ · JULIE BISHOP · JAMES HOLDEN · PETER COE · RICHARD JAECKEL

Directed by Allan Dwan · Associate Producer— Edmund Grainger

A REPUBLIC PICTURE

John Wayne never failed to entertain. He delighted audiences in his early Western *Stagecoach* (1939). He tugged at the heartstrings with his masterful portrayal of the broken but resolute Ethan Edwards in *The Searchers* (1956), and he brought the laughs with his Oscar-winning role in *True Grit* (1969). Although each of those three films undoubtedly deserve the title of masterpiece, one movie in Duke's career stands out as more than a film and much more than entertainment. *Sands of Iwo Jima* (1949) manages to capture on celluloid the bravery, determination, despair, hope and sacrifice of the Marines who put it all on the line when their country needed them most. It isn't a movie—it's a memorial to the Greatest Generation. Decades later, it still manages to fill audiences with reverence and awe.

Republic Pictures producer Edmund Grainger came up with the idea for the film while reading the newspaper, and the phrase "sands of Iwo Jima" leapt from the page to spark a firestorm of creativity in the movie mogul's brain. After crafting a bare-bones plot outline—a strict Marine sergeant molds the men under his command into warriors able to withstand the horrors of combat— Grainger eventually landed a $1 million budget (the largest for any Republic movie at the time), and he cast John Wayne in the starring role. The character of Sgt. John M. Stryker constituted another high-profile part that allowed Duke to show a different side to audiences, most of which only knew him as the white hat-wearing cowboy. As Duke began pushing middle age, the actor started tackling more complicated roles such as *Red River*'s Thomas Dunson (1948) and *She Wore a Yellow Ribbon*'s Capt. Nathan Brittles (1949) with a rage and wearied melancholy, respectively. Although America emerged from the Second

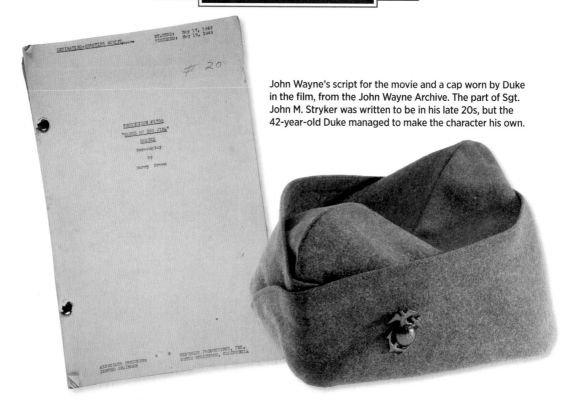

John Wayne's script for the movie and a cap worn by Duke in the film, from the John Wayne Archive. The part of Sgt. John M. Stryker was written to be in his late 20s, but the 42-year-old Duke managed to make the character his own.

World War stronger than ever, every citizen carried with him or her the wounds from that terrible conflagration, whether it was a shattered bone or a damaged psyche. Duke's newfound pathos perfectly placed him to portray Stryker, a hard-as-nails Marine and natural leader whose personal life is in tatters. It was a stunning performance that earned him his first Academy Award nomination.

Duke's spectacular on-screen work was supported by an equally impressive production. Republic Pictures had reached out to the Marine Corps in hopes of enlisting their support in creating the most realistic World War II film to date. Grainger and director Allan Dwan didn't want to just make a war movie; they wanted to redefine the genre. The Marines, for their part, were discovering their most protracted battles weren't in the fields of France or the atolls of the South Pacific but in the windowless offices of Washington bureaucrats. Certain congressional and military leaders balked at the United States

fielding two different land forces, and they campaigned to fold the Corps into the Army. As the Marines took stock of the Hollywood landscape, they determined movies glorifying the achievements of the Corps were few and far between. The decision was made to throw the dedication and effort that liberated two continents into creating the greatest war story committed to film. Republic Pictures was given full access to shoot the film at Camp Pendleton in California and was also granted use of a full battalion of Leathernecks to add to the film's epic scale. The Marines threw in their planes, tanks, artillery, Jeeps and trucks for good measure.

The Marines also helped ensure the actors carried themselves with authenticity and accuracy so as not to embarrass the Corps. Capt. Leonard Fribourg, the film's technical advisor, made sure the actors knew the lingo and wore the emblems of real Marines. The transformation of Camp Pendleton into the war-torn jungle of Iwo Jima was so complete

The recreation of Marines raising the flag over Mount Suribachi during the Battle of Iwo Jima used for the John Wayne movie. Marines planted the Stars and Stripes over the mountain twice on February 23, 1945, and while the image stands as a symbol for American might and victory, the Battle of Iwo Jima persisted for weeks after the flag-raising.

and accurate, Gen. Holland M. Smith—who commanded the American forces at the real battle of Iwo Jima (and briefly played himself in the film)—remarked to reporters: "I felt as though I were back in the South Pacific. It's so real, it's almost frightening." The Marines even left the sets up after filming to use for training exercises.

Smith wasn't the only Marine to step in front of the camera. Near the film's conclusion, three of the surviving Marines who raised the flag over Mount Suribachi—Privates First Class Rene Gagnon and Ira Hayes, as well as Pharmacist's Mate Second Class John Bradley—recreated the famous tableau once more for *Sands of Iwo Jima*. The incorporation of the three Marines marks the true success of the film, which can't be measured in the more than $5 million it earned at the box office or the Academy Award nominations it garnered. It was and continues to be measured in the respect and honor the film paid the men who gave all for their country—and how the story of their sacrifice would be preserved for future generations.

Clockwise from top left: John Wayne and Anna Lee in *Flying Tigers*, 1942; *The Longest Day*, 1962; John Wayne and Robert Montgomery in *They Were Expendable*, 1945; Duke and Ward Bond in *Operation Pacific*, 1951. The following dedication is included in the credits for *They Were Expendable*: "We hearby tender our deep appreciation to the United States Navy, Army, Coast Guard and Office of Strategic Services whose splendid cooperation made this production possible."

Clockwise from left: Duke in *Sands of Iwo Jima*, 1949; *In Harm's Way*, 1965; Duke and Dennis O'Keefe in *The Fighting Seabees*, 1944. *The Fighting Seabees* is one of only eight movies in which Duke dies on-screen.

Clockwise from top left: Duke and Burgess Meredith in *In Harm's Way* (1965); John Wayne and Robert Ryan in *Flying Leathernecks* (1951); Tom Neal and Duke in *Flying Tigers* (1942). Preproduction titles for *Flying Tigers* included "Yanks Over the Burma Road" and "Yanks Over Singapore."

Clockwise from top left: *In Harm's Way* (1965); Duke and John Carroll in *Flying Tigers* (1942); Duke and Ward Bond in *Operation Pacific* (1951); *Back to Bataan* (1945). According to *Hollywood Citizen-News*, proceeds from the L.A. premiere of *Back to Bataan* were donated to a special war fund; John Wayne and Robert Montgomery in *They Were Expendable* (1945).

The Longest Day

In 1962, legendary producer Darryl Zanuck committed himself to creating the definitive cinematic telling of the Allied invasion of Normandy during World War II, stripped of the extraneous melodrama and superfluous subplots marring even the best war films of the era. Zanuck's nervousness over the possibility of an ill reception convinced him to cast a bevy of A-listers—including Duke as real-life Lt. Col. Benjamin Vandervoort—to increase the film's chance at commercial success. The result is not only a great John Wayne film that has Duke portraying a true American hero but also a quantum leap forward in telling realistic war stories in Hollywood—an effort that helps everyday American civilians understand the incredible toll taken on the soldiers who fought for our country.

Until *Schindler's List* claimed the title in 1993, *The Longest Day* was the most expensive black-and-white production ever made. In addition to Duke and Robert Mitchum, actors Henry Fonda, Richard Burton, Sean Connery, Red Buttons and Roddy McDowall appeared in the film along with dozens of other recognizable faces proudly representing the men who, less than 20 years earlier, had liberated Europe from fascism. Adding to the film's epic scope were an estimated 23,000 real-life soldiers used as extras.

But what separates *The Longest Day* from other Hollywood epics of the era remembered less-fondly today was the focus on the individual. The audience never doubts the courage and leadership Duke's Vandervoort displays comes from a man wrestling with grave decisions during one of the most important battles in history, and the other actors similarly shine in their roles as America's finest and bravest citizens.

John Wayne as Lt. Col. Benjamin Vandervoort in *The Longest Day* (1962). The real-life Vandervoot was awarded the Distinguished Service Cross for his valor.

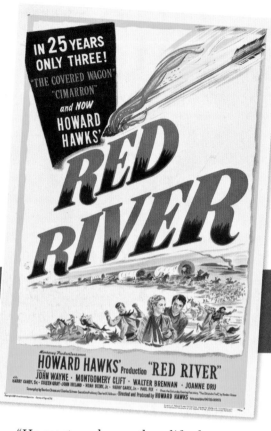

Red River

By the late 1940s, John Wayne could consider himself a bona fide box office star (and more importantly to the studio heads, a box office draw) and had some freedom to shape his career like he never had before. And in true Duke fashion, he didn't rest on his laurels. John Wayne always sought to challenge himself by taking on new roles that spoke to him and the values he stood for. With the character of Tom Dunson in director Howard Hawks's *Red River* (1948), John Wayne found a canvas upon which he could paint one of the most well-rounded arguments for the importance of values ever committed to film. Dunson isn't a white-hat-wearing angel who rides into town with a smile and a quick draw to clear out the bad guys, kiss the girl and head off into the sunset. He's a man who often acts like a tyrant to his employees and barrels headlong into what appears to be a fatal fight with his adopted adult son.

"He creates a larger-than-life character made human, and therefore sympathetic, through his flaws," says Brian Eggert, head critic of the film website Deep Focus Reviews. The story of how this flawed character copes with his beliefs and values when they're tested to their extremes makes *Red River* the ultimate John Wayne values movie—and one relatable to many Americans, especially at a time when loyalty and trust were being tested in the face of communism and the early days of the Cold War.

Part of the reason *Red River* makes such a strong statement about values can be credited to director Howard Hawks, who often gravitated toward stories about codes of living, particularly when it came to the idea of the "self-made man." Films such as 1932's *Scarface* and 1941's *Sergeant*

From left: A poster for *Red River* (1948); John Wayne as Thomas Dunson in the film. Makeup had to be applied to make Duke look older.

York tackled the idea of how an individual can achieve greatness through strength of will. Even Hawks's comedies hover around the themes of self-sufficiency. Lorelei Lee, Marilyn Monroe's character in *Gentlemen Prefer Blondes* (1953), relies on her looks and charm to carve out an ideal life for herself. It's no surprise Hawks would return time and again to the Western genre, where a character's tenacity and grit not only shapes his or her life but also the budding civilization depicted in those films.

Red River's plot centers on a cattle drive led by John Wayne's Tom Dunson, a man whose only family is his adopted son Matt Garth, played by a young Montgomery Clift. Dunson, Garth and a gang of hired hands traverse treacherous terrain on their way from Texas to Missouri, the specter of starvation haunting every step after a stampede and other assorted disasters leave them short on supplies. Dunson's harsh measures to enforce discipline on the trail include whipping one of his employees and attempting to lynch two more who deserted the group, taking with them a sack of flour.

From left: John Wayne and Montgomery Clift in a scene from *Red River*. Although Clift was an actor from a different generation than Duke and followed Lee Strasberg's "Method," both men knocked their roles out of the park; a lobby card for the film; John Wayne's copy of the *Red River* script.

←THE RED RIVER→
FIRST FINAL

AUGUST 23, 1946

"In reality, cattle drivers like Dunson needed to be hard and unflinching, sometimes even cruel, to survive," Eggert says. "They made tough decisions and, much as Dunson does, created their own rule of law." Dunson's responsibilities as a leader of men dictate he take what he considers to be necessary measures, even as Garth deems those measures an unacceptable violation of the bond between the makeshift family comprised of the men on the trail. "*Red River* demonstrates that it takes a family to take on a drive," Eggert says. "Some people in the family may be willing to make the hard calls, while others look after the welfare of its members. But without its key members looking after the entire family unit, it falls apart." And fall apart it does, culminating in Dunson tracking down Garth (who has taken control of the cattle drive and guided them to Abilene, Kansas) and engaging in a no-holds-barred brawl. But it isn't a fight to the death. The two men reconcile, and it means more than a happy ending. It's a statement about how even when our values pull us in conflicting directions, they'll see us through our most trying moments. "This is how Hawks saw America," Eggert says. "He saw self-made men struggling through impossible odds and coming out stronger on the other end; he saw frontiersmen carving out a slice of the West for themselves; he saw America built on sometimes awful behavior and the willingness to move beyond that and improve." That sentiment was just as true in the Old West as it was when John Wayne made *Red River* in 1948—and it still holds up today.

She Wore A Yellow Ribbon

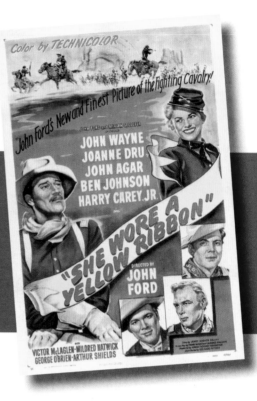

When John Wayne and John Ford combined their artistic talents, they proved time and again that they were capable of creating some of the most profound statements about American history, legacy and the individual—themes perfectly explored through stories of soldiers and combat. Although the plot of *She Wore a Yellow Ribbon* (1949) takes place decades before World War II, the questions it raises couldn't have been more relevant to an audience that had just emerged from that global conflict. Can the opportunity of a fresh start inspire people to change? At what point do the traditions that define us weigh us down? Do the pioneers who lay the foundation for a society later have a place in it? Ford's 1949 middle entry of his Cavalry Trilogy examines through the lens of Duke's Capt. Nathan Brittles what it means to spend a life committed to an ideal, and what becomes of that life when service is no

longer required. "It's a film about maturity and old age," says Joseph McBride, film historian and author of *Searching for John Ford*. "Ford has always mourned the passage of time in his films."

In *She Wore a Yellow Ribbon*, the audience sees that passage literally marked by Capt. Brittles, a Cavalry officer who counts the days down on his wall calendar to his mandatory retirement. It's 1876, and despite Gen. Custer's crushing defeat at the Battle of Little Bighorn, the movie takes place in a West that has been more-or-less won for settlers. Brittles receives orders to lead his troop on one last mission to deal with Native American warriors on the rampage following Custer's defeat. He also finds himself saddled with transporting his commanding officer's wife Abby Allshard (played by Mildred Natwick) and niece Olivia Dandridge (played

From left: A poster for *She Wore a Yellow Ribbon*; a still of John Wayne as Capt. Brittles in the movie. The role was one of Duke's personal favorites.

From left: Duke in a scene from the film; John Wayne's script for *She Wore a Yellow Ribbon* that he used during filming, from the John Wayne Archive.

DUKE...EXHIBITS THE MIXTURE OF PRIDE, REGRET AND WISDOM OF A MAN DECADES OLDER.

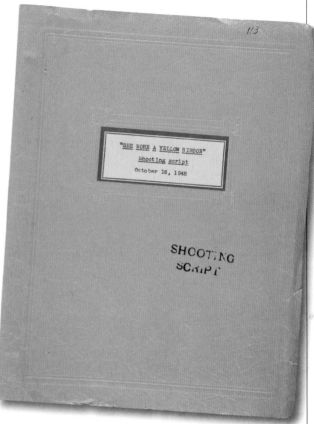

by Joanne Dru) to a stagecoach where they'll flee to relative safety, a complication that creates tension among two of Brittle's junior officers competing for the niece's romantic affections.

The movie's plot can generously be described as shaggy, bordering on cryptic. "Ford disliked scenes with exposition, which forced the audience to use their intelligence to follow the plot," McBride says. But the film's soul lies with the scenes between Brittles and the men and women who have become family to him, such as First Sgt. Quincannon (played by Victor McLaglen). Watching Brittles smell Quincannon's breath for the whiff of whiskey in the morning or give a heartfelt talk about leadership to one of his younger officers establishes a history that makes Brittles's impending retirement that much more heart wrenching. "The most moving part of *She Wore a Yellow Ribbon* is the scene when he's saying farewell to his troops," McBride says.

And while credit should go to the movie's writers, James Warner Bellah (who wrote the stories the script was based on) and screenwriters Frank S. Nugent and Laurence Stallings, John Wayne and his performance play the indispensable role in selling the pathos of Brittles's story. Although Duke was only in his early 40s while filming *She Wore a Yellow Ribbon*, he effortlessly exhibits the mixture of pride, regret and wisdom of a man decades older.

The role of Brittles also allowed John Wayne to show a softer, gentler side to his persona hinted at in earlier roles such as *Stagecoach*'s the Ringo Kid. The captain isn't a hellbent killer or hotheaded gunslinger. Brittles serves more as a father figure for the rest of his troop, and scenes such as one in which he talks to his deceased wife at her grave allow John Wayne to sink his teeth into one of the most well-rounded roles in his career.

"Brittles is such a rich and compelling character for Wayne," says McBride. "The hesitation with which he reads some of his lines and his facial expressions shows Brittles as someone who is vulnerable. He should have won an Oscar for the role." But the only person from *She Wore a Yellow Ribbon* who walked away with Oscar gold was cinematographer Winton Hoch. It's difficult to argue with the decision after watching how the gorgeous vistas of Monument Valley were captured for the movie, giving an epic scope to a personal story. For years after its theatrical run, the only surviving format of *She Wore a Yellow Ribbon* was in black-and-white, robbing audiences of one of the Technicolor era's greatest masterpieces. It wasn't until an effort spearheaded by UCLA that the film was restored to its vibrant colors.

No matter whether audiences see the movie in color or black-and-white, John Ford's strong opinions on how to find

meaning during life's twilight years are crystal clear. Toward the end of the film, Brittles rides off into the sunset and into his new life as a civilian. But the last-minute intervention of the Army brass sees Brittles receive a promotion and new posting as chief of scouts of the Cavalry. It's the happy ending Ford hoped for himself and his compatriots who served the country in World War II—a continuing legacy of service and usefulness even after one's halcyon days have passed.

From left: One of the last scenes of the movie where Duke's Capt. Brittles is paid tribute; John Wayne and Chief John Big Tree, who played Chief Pony That Walks in the movie.

Servicemen show off a battle trophy to Duke (far right) and singer Benjamin De Louche (far left). The saber was taken from a Japanese officer killed in battle on Cape Gloucester.

Duke leads a charge for freedom as Col. Joseph Madden in *Back to Bataan* (1945). Behind the scenes, Col. George Clarke of the U.S. Army (who had participated in the actual Battle of Bataan) ensured the film was as realistic as possible.

Duke in *The Longest Day* (1962).
A colorized version of the film
was released in 1994, on the 50th
anniversary of D-Day.

American Ad Man

Our country's values and freedoms may make us strong, but our prosperity is the beating heart that keeps the American Dream going. Nobody believed in that dream more than John Wayne, and the actor knew behind every billboard advertisement and commercial jingle was a product made by American workers in American factories. When Duke agreed to an endorsement, he was doing more than just picking up a check for himself and his family— he was helping the average worker grab his piece of prosperity.

French's Worcestershire Sauce *c. 1947*

Adam Hats *c. 1940*

Royal Crown Cola *c. 1948*

THE STEREO Realist
(the camera that puts 3rd dimension on film)

is preferred by people who know picture taking and picture making

Ektachrome by Bert Six

Stars of "BIG JIM McLAIN", A Wayne-Fellows Production released by Warner Bros.

John Wayne and Nancy Olson say:

"Take it easy . . . with Stereo-REALIST. It is amazing how simple this camera is to operate. And it takes the most beautiful, true-to-life pictures we've ever seen."

There's no doubt about it—Stereo-REALIST takes the kind of pictures you've always wanted. They're beautiful beyond description, with full, natural color and thrilling, *realistic* three dimensions.

What's more, the REALIST is so *easy* to use that people who never before owned a camera get outstanding pictures on their very first roll of film. It's economical, too, producing 29 stereo pairs from a 36-exposure roll of 35 mm. film.

You have to see REALIST pictures to fully appreciate their exciting beauty. Ask your camera dealer to show you some. Once you do, you'll agree that the REALIST is the ideal camera for your personal pleasure . . . and to use as a sales tool in your business. DAVID WHITE COMPANY, 505 W. Court Street, Milwaukee 12, Wisconsin.

$139.00
(Tax Inc.)

STEREO Realist

THE CAMERA THAT SEES THE SAME AS YOU

Cameras, Viewers, Projectors and Accessories are products of the David White Company, Milwaukee 12, Wisconsin.

Stereo Realist Cameras *c. 1952*

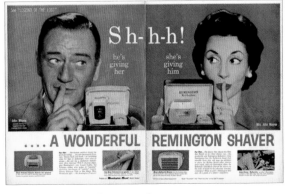

Melinda Wayne, pictured with Duke, Patrick, Toni and Michael at the Los Angeles Rodeo. Melinda remembers telling her father she wanted a car in high school and John Wayne telling her she would have to work during the summer to earn money for it. "I saved all my money," says Melinda. "Then, the day of my graduation comes, and he hands me a box with a key to a car in it. I tried to give him my money, but he said no, to use it for insurance and gas. He was trying to teach me to be responsible."

With a little support from Marine Pvt. Inga Boberg and Sid Grauman, Duke leaves his footprint in front of the famous Grauman's Chinese Theatre, 1950. Though many celebrities only leave hand or footprints, Duke also included his fist.

★1950–1960★
THE DECADE OF DUKE

JOHN WAYNE started off the '50s with a bang, putting out the final installment of director John Ford's "cavalry trilogy," *Rio Grande*, as well as receiving a star on Hollywood's Walk of Fame. Over the next 10 years Duke also made *The Quiet Man*, *Hondo*, *The Searchers* and *Rio Bravo*, and in 1960, he capped off this 10-year span of success with *The Alamo*. The rest of America was having a good decade, too: The baby boom was in full swing, the economy was on the rise, television was sweeping the nation—it seemed the good times would go on forever.

With the U.S. population exploding, Americans weren't satisfied with living packed together cheek-to-jowl in their now too-small housing. To keep up with the demand for more expansive and comfortable living space, developers such as William Levitt began mass-producing tract housing around the nation. In New York, New Jersey and Pennsylvania, his "Levittowns" became iconic symbols of American suburban life. Suburban living proved popular: According to an October 1981 issue of *Domestic*

An aerial view of a housing tract in Levittown, Pennsylvania, c. 1957. Between 1952 and 1958, more than 17,000 homes were built in this development.

Engineering, "Three out of five families became homeowners, and suburban living became a national phenomenon."

A healthy real estate market was just one symptom of an overall strong economy. The gross national product increased dramatically in the 15 years after WWII, from $200 billion in 1945 to $500 billion in 1960. This was largely due to government spending, including hard-earned veteran's benefits, an increase in military spending and investments in the construction of interstate highways and schools.

What's more, the expansion of new businesses meant consumers had more choices than ever before. Big business quickly realized the burgeoning baby boomers were a vast, untapped market and set to work creating an attractive line of toys and games that would define a generation's dreams.

Children were suddenly able to ask their parents for Frisbees, Barbie dolls, Slinkys, Magic 8 Balls and more. And there wasn't a shortage of options for adults, either, who had a slew of new big-ticket items to choose from, such as cars and color televisions.

Television programming had existed as a mostly regional oddity through World War II, limited to 15-minute newscasts and a few barely decipherable sporting events available to the few users living near major metropolitan areas such as New York or Los Angeles. After the Allies emerged victorious and industry in America could pivot from a wartime footing, television production and ownership blossomed in the country. In 1946, only about 6,000 television sets were in use in the U.S. By 1951 that number had climbed to 12 million, statistical evidence of Americans' hunger for the new medium.

The 1950s saw the three major television networks—NBC, CBS and ABC—solidify a regular broadcasting schedule beginning with programs mostly lifted from radio, the far more established form of mass media. Shows such as *The Lone Ranger*, *The Gene Autry Show* and *Truth and Consequences* were among the many popular programs with roots in radio. Creators also favored anthology-style "teleplays"—small dramas that were little more than televised theater productions.

As the decade marched on, television producers realized having their programs stick with a set of recurring characters was not only less of a hassle to organize for weekly shows but also what audiences preferred. Situational comedies such as *I Love Lucy* and *The Adventures of Ozzie and Harriet*, as well as Western dramas such as *Cheyenne* and *Gunsmoke* (introduced to audiences with a message from none other than Duke himself), began dominating the medium to the country's delight.

People didn't just gather around the television to watch Ralph Kramden threaten to send Alice to the moon or Matt Dillon gun down one of Dodge City's endless outlaws. In 1952, Americans were able to watch the major party conventions for the presidential race for the first time on television, and politics would only become more enmeshed with the medium over the years. One of the most dramatic examples of how television changed politics was the first Nixon-Kennedy presidential debate in September 1960. Nixon, who was running a low fever and sporting a five-o'clock shadow, looked haggard compared to the youthful, handsome Kennedy, who beamed from the podium like a bronzed Bostonian god. In polls after the debate, Americans who listened to the candidates on the radio gave the advantage to Nixon or called it a draw. But those watching on television called the debate for Kennedy, a clear indicator that in the years ahead, politicians would have to think even more like actors to win over the public's trust.

John F. Kennedy and Richard Nixon debate on live television, 1960. When discussing the debate in his memoir *Six Crises*, Nixon wrote, "I should have remembered that 'a picture is worth a thousand words.'"

A Hidden Gem

John Wayne may have loved every inch of this country, from the sleepy hamlets of New England to the Rocky Mountains of the West, but a few locations found a special place in Duke's heart. The white beaches of Hawaii was one such place, where he married his wife Pilar and enjoyed countless vacations, as was the idyllic town of Newport Beach, California, where he made his home. But in Monument Valley, located in the expansive sprawl of the American Southwest, Duke found something more than just a setting for some of his most beloved films. He discovered a vision of the country's majestic beauty, which is shared with audiences every time they watch *She Wore a Yellow Ribbon* (1949), *Rio Grande* (1950), *The Searchers* (1956) and other classics filmed in the area.

Though most people might be familiar with the haunting allure of the valley from its many appearances on the silver screen throughout the decades, it's been home to visitors and inhabitants long before the invention of cinema. Monument Valley, an expanse of 91,696 acres within a Navajo tribal area, extends into both Utah and Arizona. The handful of Navajo who continue to make a living herding and farming on the valley floor stand as a testament to how the valley's isolation has helped preserve both its natural beauty and its people. During America's great march westward under the banner of Manifest

John Wayne with some impressive armaments in hand in a scene from *The Searchers* (1956).

Duke astride a horse in a scene from *Fort Apache* (1948).

Destiny, the relative inhospitality of the valley protected it from permanent development, but it failed to prevent the U.S. Army from driving out the Native inhabitants (the Navajos were allowed to return in 1868). The area's rugged splendor remained relatively hidden to the outside world until the 1920s, when an entrepreneurial and resilient trader named Harry Goulding set up a two-story shack with his wife in the area. His aim was to use his humble residence as a trading outpost for the Navajos who still resided in their ancestral home. When Mother Nature afflicted Monument Valley with a devastating drought, drying up not only water but also commerce between Goulding and his customers, the native Coloradan decided to make a pilgrimage of more than 600 miles to Hollywood in a last-ditch effort to preserve his livelihood and the well-being of his customers. According to later stories, Goulding marched himself right to the offices of United Artists—one of the largest players

in Tinseltown's dream factory—armed with an album of photos of the valley, a bedroll and a determination as solid and unmoving as the rocks of his home. Goulding wanted to talk to someone about using the valley as a film location, and the irresistible force of the old homesteader eventually overcame the seemingly immovable object of studio system bureaucracy. Goulding was eventually granted a meeting with director John Ford, who was won over by the cinematic potential he saw in Goulding's photographs. Ford

John Wayne in a film still from *The Searchers*. Shooting in Monument Valley resembled an intense camping trip, with the cast doubling up in cabins and sharing a single shower.

decided to film his new movie *Stagecoach* (1939) in Monument Valley, and audiences of the breakthrough film were able to share in Ford and Goulding's appreciation for the weathered landscape. Theatergoers weren't the only ones to benefit from how Ford and Duke adopted the valley as their go-to location for making Westerns. Hollywood crews on long shoots meant an influx of people needing to be fed, sheltered and entertained while they weren't working. Goulding's business boomed, and his outpost eventually morphed into the hotel and store, Goulding's Lodge, that is still in business. Ford also gave an economic assist to the local Navajos, with hires ranging from the pedestrian (paying Navajos to fill in as extras in his films) to the bizarre (paying a medicine man $15 a day to bring about ideal weather for shooting film). Over time, John Wayne, John Ford and their crew would continue to be a welcome sight in the valley—just as the landscape has been a wonder to behold for audiences then, now and in the future.

Working for Himself

The American Dream takes on as many different forms as there are citizens of this nation, but the idea of founding and building up a business of one's own surely qualifies as one of the more popular iterations of the dream. By the late 1940s, John Wayne had just begun to enjoy the popularity and opportunities he had worked for decades to achieve, but the actor was already scanning the horizons for his next challenge. Not satisfied with just delivering commanding performances in front of the camera, Duke dove headfirst into Hollywood's least glamorous side—sorting through the raw material of Hollywood's dream machine and producing the right pieces into films. "If you gave him an opportunity, he took advantage of it," Patrick Wayne told author Michael Goldman for the book *The Genuine Article.* "He would develop it and work on it. He never took anything for granted. His life was based on hard work and preparation and more preparation and hard work. He never stopped learning or being curious, and he was always trying to improve himself."

John Wayne first stretched this particular set of managerial muscles with Republic Pictures' *Angel and the Badman* (1947), for which he received a producer credit. He produced *The Fighting Kentuckian* two years later, in addition to several short films for Sid Davis Productions and another feature

for Republic, 1951's *Bullfighter and the Lady.* The latter film, starring Robert Stack as a braggadocious American who travels to Spain and picks up bullfighting to impress a woman, earned an Academy Award nomination for Best Story (an award that was phased out in 1957 in favor of Best Original Screenplay).

By 1952, Duke had formally partnered with Robert Fellows, a producer at RKO Radio pictures with whom he had worked before, to form Wayne/Fellows Productions (the company was renamed Batjac in 1956 after Fellows sold his shares).

Right out of the gate, the new production company made clear they would make films taking advantage of John Wayne's star power in unusual ways. The first film, *Big Jim McLain* (1952), cast Duke as a rough and rugged lawman, but one who hunted suspected communists in contemporary Hawaii instead of bandits in the Old West. It wasn't until the company's fourth film, 1953's *Hondo,* that audiences saw John Wayne in his accustomed habitat of the Western frontier. "His vision, I suppose, for Batjac was to provide good entertainment with interesting characters, work with writers he was comfortable with…and make a return on his investment," Gretchen Wayne, Duke's daughter-in-law through son Michael and current president of Batjac, told Turner Classic Movies. "I don't think he ever used public

From left: John Wayne's Batjac business cards, from the John Wayne Archive; during production of 1954's *The High and the Mighty*, Duke stops for a cup of coffee with producer Robert Fellows. The film sees passengers aboard a plane recall their lives before a crash landing.

interest as a bellwether for his selections. Most important was good family entertainment."

That's not to say the films produced by Batjac were all little-seen gems. On the contrary, many of the movies have found a place in the hearts of Duke's fans as his best-remembered movies. Films such as *The Alamo* (1960)—which John Wayne produced, directed and starred in—and *McLintock!* (1963) prove Duke's creative sensibilities both behind and in front of the camera connected with audiences—the

entire reason he founded his own production company. The company also allowed Duke to work more with the people he trusted best. Duke's eldest son Michael produced *McLintock!*, providing him with his first opportunity to direct his father. "He was 27 years old and given the opportunity to produce a John Wayne film, which was, indeed, a big thrill and challenge," Gretchen told TCM. "He brought it in under budget and ahead of schedule, and it was tremendously successful. It came out just after John F. Kennedy was

From left: John Wayne, Randolph Scott and Budd Boetticher on the set of *Seven Men From Now* (1956), a Batjac production that explores the classic Western theme of the aftermath of a stagecoach robbery; boxes from Batjac Productions dated from the 1950s, from the John Wayne Archive.

"HIS VISION, I SUPPOSE, FOR BATJAC WAS TO PROVIDE GOOD ENTERTAINMENT WITH INTERESTING CHARACTERS...."

about the conflict in Southeast Asia that turned out to be a winner at the box office. For John Wayne, the hit film was just another vindication of his decision to trust his instincts and seize an opportunity not many had the bravery to pursue.

Batjac productions was Duke's modest contribution to the American Dream, showing his fans and future generations alike that America's greatest benefit is the ability to shape one's own destiny in one's own way, whether that meant striking out on a cattle drive or enacting a daring rescue, or in his own case, telling the inspiring stories of those who did.

assassinated. The country was looking for a little levity, and *McLintock!* filled the void of a country's sorrow."

Confident in the team he had assembled at Batjac, Duke used the company to tell stories that otherwise may have never seen the light of day. *The Green Berets* (1968), a war film centered on the heroism of American troops in Vietnam, wasn't the type of film most Hollywood moguls were rushing to make. But Duke's steadfast support of the project resulted in a unique cinematic statement

Gallery of Greatness

Big Jim McLain *1952*

When John Wayne founded Wayne/Fellows Productions in 1952, he assumed an almost-unprecedented amount of control over his career. While the 1960s and '70s would see actors found their own production companies to varying degrees of success, John Wayne leapt headfirst into the business side of a Hollywood still under the sway of the old studio system. When Robert Fellows and Duke parted ways, the actor wanted to rename the company "Batjak" after the fictional shipping company in *Wake of the Red Witch* (1948). A typo by a secretary christened the company Batjac instead, and the name stuck.

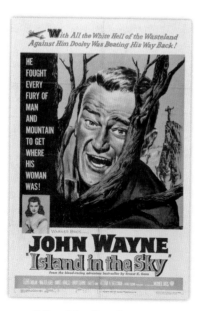

Island in the Sky *1953*

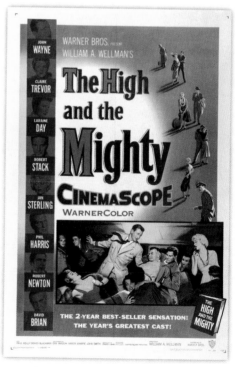

The High and the Mighty *1954*

Hondo *1953*

Blood Alley *1955*

Legend of the Lost *1957*

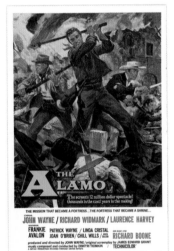

The Alamo *1960*

McLintock! *1963*

The War Wagon *1967*

The Green Berets *1968*

Chisum *1970*

Rio Lobo *1970*

The Searchers

In 1956, the master of the Western motion picture, John Ford, released his magnum opus, which also starred the physical embodiment of the Western spirit: John Wayne. Based on a true story, *The Searchers* reveals the sometimes-seedy history of the American Old West and the ever-present grit and determination embodied by our country's best citizens. Eager to do justice to the tale, both men dedicated their considerable talents and abilities to making *The Searchers* a film worth watching. "There's so much depth of emotion in this film that there's no mistaking what John Ford and John Wayne both put into it," says film historian Leonard Maltin. "The movie deals with such fundamental emotions, and that gives the film so much power." While today most critics acknowledge Ford's stunning film—based on a novel by Alan Le May and adapted to the screen by Frank S. Nugent—as one of cinema's most arresting stories, the movie originally received mixed reviews. Duke finally took home Oscar gold for his portrayal of Rooster Cogburn in *True Grit*, but bringing to life the troubled

and nuanced character of Ethan Edwards, for many, stands as John Wayne's single greatest accomplishment as an actor. In the film, Edwards stands apart from his brother Aaron and his family, yet when a Comanche raid on the farm wipes out his kin with the exception of his adopted nephew, Martin (played by Jeffrey Hunter), and his two nieces, Lucy and Debbie, who go missing, Edwards dedicates himself completely to retrieving the girls. *The Searchers* may seem like another story where the stoic, loner cowboy embarks on a righteous quest to protect his loved ones, but as Edwards's journey wears on and the bodies pile up, the character displays a dark side uncommon in most of Duke's movies. "You see the anger of the character, his hatred and desperation," says Maltin. "It's such a wide range of feelings." Even more disturbing, Edwards clearly intends to kill the grown Debbie (played by Natalie Wood) after discovering she's been raised a Comanche, a huge perversion in Edwards's eyes. Edwards's change of heart leads to one of the film's most emotional and legendary lines: "Let's go home, Debbie,"

Duke pulled off one of his most complicated and moving performances with the role of Ethan Edwards. In the film's last scene, Duke stood with his left arm grabbing his right, a call-out to silent film idol and personal role model Harry Carey Sr. Left: A half sheet for *The Searchers*.

The moving scene of Duke's Ethan Edwards cradling Debbie (played by Natalie Wood) as they return to the safety of their family. Wood's younger sister, Lana, played Debbie during the scenes where she was a child.

From left: The rag doll Debbie leaves behind after the massacre; John Wayne's personal record of the film's theme song, "Song of the Prodigal"; and his copy of the 1954 book by Alan Le May, from the John Wayne Archive.

and the audience can hear the character let go of years of hate and revenge, thanks to Duke's pitch-perfect delivery.

The legacy of *The Searchers* lives on in American auteurs whom the film inspired, including Martin Scorsese and Steven Spielberg. And the film has influenced the small screen, too. "When my writers and I were outlining our final episode of *Breaking Bad*, we came up with a plot twist which made us all exceedingly proud," says Vince Gilligan, creator of the critically acclaimed television drama. "At that point in the story, our main character, Walter White, hated his partner, Jesse Pinkman, and planned on killing him at their next meeting. But once Walt finally laid eyes on the young man, he saw how victimized his partner had become and had a silent change of heart. We were very

proud of this stunningly original plot twist we had concocted, until it dawned on me that this same twist ends *The Searchers*," Gilligan continued. "Writers and directors like me—if we're smart—will continue to be inspired by the work of John Ford (and Alan Le May and Frank S. Nugent) for centuries to come."

Although *The Searchers* is more than 60 years old, Duke's most riveting and unforgettable role hasn't faded. Cleverly weaving a nuanced portrayal of a tumultuous period in America's history with gorgeous, sweeping views of her landscapes, it's no wonder Duke (and *The Searchers*) is remembered so fondly. In fact, in 1989, it became one of the first films selected by the National Film Preservation Board as an American movie with strong cultural significance.

Lassoing in the Living Room

On September 10, 1955, Americans watching their televisions across the country were treated to a personal address by none other than Duke himself. At the height of his celebrity, John Wayne made what was at the time an unusual appearance on the small screen to introduce the first episode of a new, adult Western series called *Gunsmoke*. "No I'm not in it," John Wayne told audiences. "I wish I were though. 'Cause I think it's the best thing of its kind that's come along." In fact, Duke actually played a key role in making sure friend and actor James Arness landed the role of *Gunsmoke's* lead, Marshal Matt Dillon. Arness was under contract to the icon's production company, but when CBS offered Arness the role, Duke gladly freed him of his legal obligation and encouraged his friend to seize the opportunity. Duke (as usual) proved to have a good eye for business—*Gunsmoke* ran on CBS for 20 years. Clocking in 635 episodes, it's the record holder for the longest-running, live-action show in the United States. In short, it became an American institution, and one whose birth Duke witnessed firsthand. *Gunsmoke* was the Western's most successful foray into a new media frontier that would ensure the genre's popularity for generations to come. By the 1958–1959 television season, seven of the top 10 most watched programs were Westerns, a clear sign that the appeal of the stories John Wayne starred in could be translated into the more modest budgets and production values of TV.

Gunsmoke wasn't the first Western to grace television screens, but much like *Seinfeld* revolutionized the sitcom and *The Sopranos* the hour-long drama, this Western raised Americans' expectations for their entertainment. Prior to *Gunsmoke*, most televised Westerns catered more to children than their parents. Programs such as *The Gene Autry Show, Hopalong Cassidy* and *The Lone Ranger* all took square aim at the after-school crowd with their simple adventure plots to make them more resemble cartoons than anything in which John Wayne would star. *Gunsmoke* and its cohorts (such as *Cheyenne* and *Have Gun—Will Travel*) endeavored to bring to television stories populated by characters driven by realistic motivations and desires and whose conflicts couldn't always be solved by a punch or a bullet— though they often were. "This term 'adult Western' came in and was overused, but the fact is that's what [*Gunsmoke*] was," actor James Arness, who played Marshal Matt Dillon on *Gunsmoke* for all 20 of its seasons, told the *Archive of American Television* in 2002. "[Dillon] hated violence, particularly shooting. If Matt Dillon had to shoot somebody, you'd cut around to him. You could see that he just hated to have to

John Wayne introduces the first episode of *Gunsmoke*, 1955. While Duke made special guest appearances on shows such as *I Love Lucy* and televised specials, he never starred as a regular on any program.

From left: Dennis Weaver as Chester Goode, Amanda Blake as Kitty Russell and James Arness as Marshal Matt Dillon in the *Gunsmoke* episode "The Thoroughbreds" from the show's fourth season, June 21, 1958. Characters from television programs became almost as familiar to many Americans as members of their own family during the 1950s, as TV became a dominant media platform.

do that, and he felt a sort of revulsion over it. That's something that hadn't really been done much up to that point."

Though the gunplay and fisticuffs featured in the televised Westerns look like child's play compared to today's displays of gore, the genre (along with police procedurals and other genres) found itself under attack from citizens concerned that the staged violence on a soundstage could foster real violence in American communities. Congress had held hearings on the subject of regulating the content of television programs since 1952, but concern reached a new height in 1961 when Newton N. Minow, Chairman of the Federal Communications Commission, denounced most of what was being broadcast as part of a "vast wasteland" in a speech to the National Association of Broadcasters.

Sensitive to the winds of change, the networks and studios spent the 1960s making sure the Westerns they aired had a more family-friendly tone, such as *Bonanza* (which actually premiered in 1959 but drew its highest ratings during the '60s) and *The Big Valley*. The stories told by these shows focused far more on jawing it out than shooting 'em up, a welcome change for those worried about their children being inundated with violent images. As the decade wore on, the Western found itself sharing space on network schedules with shows from other genres, such as the urban crime drama. By the end of the '60s, the Western's televised golden age had come to a close. However, half a century later, shows such as Netflix's *Godless* (2017–) and HBO's *Westworld* (2016–) have shown that classic American stories full of grit and gunslingers still appeal to audiences, a fact that Duke would likely be glad—though not surprised—to hear.

Duke and his wife Pilar share a kiss during their wedding in Hawaii, 1954. The couple had their first child, Aissa, about two years later.

Aloha, Pilgrim

The name "John Wayne" may bring to mind images of windswept plains and shimmering deserts, but the vibrant sands and cerulean waters of Hawaii were also prominent in the legend's life. America's youngest state became a frequent destination for Duke for occasions both professional and personal. By the end of his career and life, the island had been forever etched into the John Wayne legacy, serving as the site of some of his major milestones.

Like most Americans from the mainland, Duke fell in love with Hawaiian culture before ever stepping a foot on the islands. While filming the 1948 adventure-romance *Wake of the Red Witch* in Los Angeles, John Wayne met Hawaiian legend Duke Kahanamoku (pictured above), a five-time Olympic medalist in swimming and the man considered to be the "father of surfing." On set, the two shared the screen as John Wayne played the courageous Captain Ralls and Kahanamoku assumed the role of tribal chief Ua Nuke, but their time together off the clock would prove just as worthwhile. Already united by their love of the ocean and the sport of surfing, the two Dukes forged a close bond. With Kahanamoku as his guide, John Wayne became acquainted with Hawaiian culture, and his love for it drove the

actor to visit the tropical island many times during the '50s. Even when he was back on the mainland, John Wayne would continue in the island's easy-going spirit by spending long afternoons enjoying a drink with friends John Ford, Ward Bond and others as part of a group they informally called the Emerald Bay Yacht Club.

Duke would get his first business-related chance to return to the Big Island in 1952 for the filming of *Big Jim McLain*. Playing the titular character, an investigator tasked with hunting down communists in Hawaii, the actor was right at home in the role thanks to its patriotic nature and familiar setting. One year later, John Wayne found himself back in Hawaii co-producing and starring in *The High and the Mighty*, which filmed on location at the Royal Hawaiian Hotel and Waikiki Beach. The string of films proved Duke's unmatched charisma and Hawaii's inviting scenery were a winning combination.

The following year, the sun-soaked Kona Coast became more than a set location for the tireless icon. It was also where he

BY THE END OF HIS CAREER AND LIFE, THE ISLAND HAD BEEN FOREVER ETCHED INTO THE JOHN WAYNE LEGACY.

tied the knot with the woman he loved. On November 1, 1954, while filming the World War II action-drama *The Sea Chase* (1955), John Wayne married Peruvian actress Pilar Pallete, whom he had met two years prior on a trip to Tingo María, Peru. The wedding was held at Territorial Senator William H. Hill's summer home, which was also the former home of Hawaiian King Kamehameha III. Duke resumed shooting on the island following his nuptials, but the couple spent their free time dining on exotic foods, swimming through the scenic waters and relaxing on seemingly endless beaches.

By the early 1960s, Duke was a regular around the Aloha State, where he placed a fitting capstone on his professional relationship with director John Ford. In 1962, Ford summoned Duke to star in the action-comedy *Donovan's Reef*, a collaboration that would ultimately be their last. The film's fun-loving feel—particularly the on-screen camaraderie between John Wayne's "Guns" Donovan and costar Lee Marvin's "Boats" Gilhooley—perfectly represents the time Duke and Ford spent together in their 35 years as co-workers and close friends.

John Wayne filmed one final movie in Hawaii in 1964, *In Harm's Way* (1965). It was a cinematic farewell to the charming, idyllic American paradise that was so near and dear to the icon's heart.

Duke and son Michael on a Hawaiian beach. Michael produced many of his father's movies starting in 1963.

John Wayne plays a game of catch with some of his dogs outside his San Fernando Valley home in 1952. Duke sold the home in 1964 to Walt Disney's oldest daughter and her family.

Laurence Harvey, Richmard Widmark and Duke stand in front of a crowd of extras in a scene from *The Alamo* (1960).

The Alamo

By the beginning of the 1950s, John Wayne had already been a mainstay in the movie industry for more than two decades. He worked his way up from the depths of B-movies and serials to the lofty peaks of A-list stardom, headlining classics such as *Back to Bataan* (1945), *Angel and the Badman* (1947) and *Red River* (1948), to name a few. Duke had accomplished more than most actors ever do, but the hardworking star wasn't one to simply rest on his laurels. As the smoke cleared from the battlefields of World War II and Americans slowly recovered from the horror of that conflict, John Wayne felt a calling to take his art to the next level in service of a generation that helped secure freedom at home and peace abroad. The biggest name in Hollywood would spend more than a decade trying to bring his dream, a film enshrining the ideals of this nation and the sacrifices sometimes required to preserve them, into cinematic reality. The result, 1960's *The Alamo*, "is an emotional reminder of what we respect—liberty, freedom and independence," says John Farkis, author of *Not Thinkin'...Just Rememberin'...The Making of John Wayne's The Alamo*, a comprehensive oral history of the Western epic he spent years researching and compiling. The movie may not be placed in the same league as *The Searchers* (1956) or *The Quiet Man* (1952), but what it does accomplish is preserving a cinematic love letter from America's greatest actor to the country that gave him so much.

John Wayne never wavered in his belief that *The Alamo* was an important film America needed, but he had difficulty

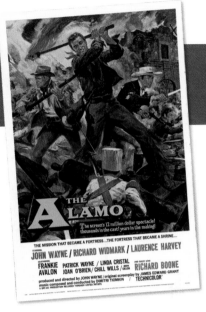

From top: A poster for *The Alamo*; a prop gun from the film signed by Duke for a Marlin Rowe. Included with the rifle was a note from John Wayne's secretary, Pat Stacy, dated June 10, 1975, saying Duke would be happy to sign the prop.

convincing the movie studios of the profitability of his vision. He first started seriously pursuing the idea with Republic Pictures in the late 1940s, but Duke's insistence on directing and producing his passion project made potential backers nervous. "Though John Wayne was a fabulous actor and a box office money-maker, he was unknown as a director," Farkis says. "He thought he might just play a cameo in *The Alamo*, but the studios insisted he be one of the three major stars in the film." In 1956, John Wayne finally struck a deal with United Artists, which agreed to distribute and partially fund the prospective movie in return for Duke starring in *The Alamo* and three subsequent films. Combined with

the investments made by individuals—including several Texan businessmen eager to have Duke at the helm of the Lone Star State's most-celebrated story—and his own personal contribution, John Wayne was ready to get started.

As difficult as it was for John Wayne to get the necessary funding, the true challenge had only begun. Duke didn't set out to make just another Western—he wanted to craft a film as epic and expansive as his love for America. *The Alamo*'s budget would climb to $12 million before calling it a wrap, an astronomical figure at the time. "Most films at the time had a budget of $3 to $5 million maximum," Farkis says. "This was one of the most expensive films ever made up to that time." Part of the high costs stemmed from the army of actors, extras and the less-glamorous—but very necessary—personnel Duke hired for the production. Around 340 people were part of the cast and crew, not to mention the 1,600 horses and the 45 members of the catering service needed to feed everyone. But John Wayne's most ambitious endeavor was the construction of the set, known as Alamo Village, in Brackettville,

Texas. "It was a practical set, meaning that you could film inside the buildings. There were no false fronts," Farkis says. "This was a massive undertaking." The village, taking up 400 acres of Texas real estate, required more than one and a half million adobe bricks before its buildings were complete, including a to-scale size replica of the Alamo Mission itself. Construction took two years between 1957 and '59, including a brief pause when Duke ran out of money and had to broker a deal with the land's owner, James Tullis "Happy" Shahan, to complete construction (Shahan acquired the right to lend out the village for other movies). But for John Wayne, creating his own movie set meant he wouldn't have to rent a studio soundstage and place himself at the mercy of another's schedule. "He could film whenever, wherever and however he wanted," Farkis says.

Duke paid a price for exerting so much control over *The Alamo*, and it wasn't always measured in dollars and cents. Taking on the roles of actor, director and producer increased the star's workload to titanic proportions, and he was forced into a constant balancing act between keeping down costs, nailing his own performance as Davy Crockett and making sure the scenes he directed conformed to the film's vision. After a long day of acting and directing under the blazing Texas sun, Duke would return to his home in Fort Clark for a brief respite in the form of a massage and dinner before poring over the dailies, preparing the next day's shoot and making sure the project's finances were in order. Even after mentor John Ford showed up to lend a hand, John Wayne faced a task that would have utterly broken lesser men. But this was Duke. "The next day, he was up bright and early," Farkis says. "He was always the first one on the set and the last one to leave."

Clockwise from left: A fringed jacket made for Duke to wear in the movie; mugs Duke had made as gifts for the cast and crew; a news release of the film featuring photos and illustrations for publicity purposes; a trophy presented to John Wayne by The National Cowboy Hall of Fame and Western Heritage Museum for Outstanding Western Motion Picture in 1960. Opposite: Duke cuts into a cake depicting The Alamo Mission.

After two years of filming, John Wayne was ready to show his epic to the world. He carried in his heart not just the pride of having accomplished a feat of Herculean effort, but one that carried sky-high expectations, as well.

Duke tasked Russell Birdwell, the publicist responsible for the campaign behind *Gone With the Wind* (1939), to spread the good word about *The Alamo*. The experienced publicist went about his work in an aggressive manner, bombarding trade publications such as *Daily Variety* with ads strongly suggesting members of the Academy of Motion Picture Arts and Sciences who didn't cast a vote for *The Alamo* lacked a true love for the red, white and blue. "Once Wayne realized what Birdwell

was doing, he told him to dial the campaign back a little," Farkis says. Of the seven Oscar nominations the film received, it won only an award for Best Sound. Audiences were kinder, however, and *The Alamo* managed to eventually break even. Duke himself didn't make a dime from the film, but he still counted himself richer for the experience of creating it. What sustained John Wayne through the movie's hellish shooting schedule wasn't the dream of adding zeros to his bank account or picking up an Oscar—it was making a fitting tribute to the American values of freedom and sacrifice. "He wanted to send that message out to the world," Farkis says, "and it comes through loud and clear."

Women march for their rights in New York during the 1960s. In 1964 the Civil Rights Act was passed, protecting women from gender discrimination in the workplace.

★1960–1967★
PIONEERING A NEW FRONTIER

T HOUGH THE 1950s were largely a time of economic growth and prosperity, the boom didn't reach all demographics equally. Women and African-Americans generally had a difficult time accessing higher education: Both groups had fewer options than white men, as many colleges were segregated, and men often received enrollment preference over women. Additionally, African-Americans were often refused loans at local banks or prohibited from moving into the new suburban neighborhoods. As a result of this (and decades of prior discrimination), the 1960s were a period of societal unrest, marked by protests, sit-ins, boycotts and marches on the capital.

At the same time, tensions with the Soviet Union remained high. The battle between capitalism and communism played out in every arena imaginable, from politics to the arts and, of course, science. On October 4, 1957, Russians launched Sputnik, the first manmade object to be placed in orbit. Americans had been unprepared for the Soviets to make the first move toward space, and it both challenged the American tradition of exploration and made clear that Russia's technological capabilities outpaced those of the United States. The Russians also launched the first man into orbit in 1961, raising tensions and the stakes in the Space Race.

National nerves were further frayed in 1962, when President John F. Kennedy explained to American citizens that the Soviet Union had placed nuclear missiles on Cuba, just 90 miles from U.S. shores. Though many Americans feared a nuclear war, Kennedy agreed to Soviet leader Nikita Khrushchev's terms: The missiles were removed on the promise that the U.S. would not invade Cuba.

Just 13 months later, on November 22, 1963, the assassination of President John F. Kennedy traumatized the nation. While Duke was a strong conservative, he grieved the death of Kennedy as strongly as any other American. As he stated in a letter to journalist Wayne Warga: "You didn't have to be a Kennedy fan to be decimated by his assassination. John Kennedy could have been so very good—he was just beginning to realize his responsibilities." In fact, JFK had been the first Democratic president to whom John Wayne sent a congratulatory telegram, signed from "The Loyal Opposition."

After Kennedy's death, his vice president, Lyndon Johnson, was sworn into office. Having grown up impoverished himself, Johnson recognized that even though the '50s had been an era of great prosperity for the majority of Americans, almost a fifth had a markedly different experience during those times. In 1964, during his first State of the Union address, Johnson declared war on such circumstances. "We shall not rest until that war is won," he said. "The richest nation on Earth can afford to win it. We cannot afford to lose it."

Johnson's plan promised to give "a hand up, not a hand out," launching government programs such as Medicare and Medicaid, which help elderly and low-income citizens afford health care to this day, and Head Start, which prepared low-income children for school (the program has since been expanded to also provide health and nutrition services to children of low-income families). The Civil Rights Act was also passed in 1964, in part to address discrimination in hiring policies. Altogether, Johnson's "Great Society" initiative was ambitious—and costly. It was

too expensive to be carried out as intended, especially while money was needed for the growing conflict in Vietnam.

In 1963, the situation in Vietnam was at an all time low when a coup against President Ngo Dinh Diem by a cabal of generals led to a new government in the South. Coupled with the North's attack against two U.S. destroyers in the Gulf of Tonkin the following August, the U.S. felt it had no choice but to begin direct bombing of the North if Vietnam was to remain free. Operation Rolling Thunder, which began in 1965, dropped around 643,000 tons of munitions on the North during its three-year mission. President Lyndon Johnson also ordered 100,000 ground troops to the country in 1965, followed by another 100,000 just a year later. For many Americans, the Vietnam War had begun in earnest.

Lyndon B Johnson was an educator before becoming a politician, attending Southwest Texas State Teachers College.

Duke enjoys some time on the deck of the *Wild Goose* with Marisa. The former U.S. Navy minesweeper became a second home for John Wayne and his family.

Father Knows Best

John Wayne may have been a larger-than-life icon to the millions who watched his movies, but he was also a role model in a much more intimate way to his family, extolling classic American values at every opportunity.

Marisa Wayne, the actor's youngest daughter, recalls how the family's boat, the *Wild Goose*, played the setting for countless good times that brought Duke and his children together. "We were fishing and swimming," Marisa says. "He loved playing games, so we would play backgammon and poker. He was teaching me how to beat his friends at poker as an 8-year-old!" But Duke also found the time to teach his daughter more than cards. "There was one instance on the boat where he kept telling me to pick up my room," Marisa says. "I had clothes all over the floor. And after asking me about five times, I woke up to him throwing everything overboard." The young girl immediately dove into the water to claim her belongings, prompting Duke to ask some crew members to help her retrieve the clothes. "That was the only time where I felt the punishment was harder on him than me," Marisa laughs. "But I learned my lesson. It all came down to disrespect, and in his mind it was disrespectful that I wasn't picking up after myself. And as a parent now, I have a real hard time when one of my kids roll their eyes at me." Tough as it was for Duke, he never shirked his duties as a father, no matter how tall the task.

A Humble Home

By the 1960s, John Wayne had ascended to the pinnacle of fame and fortune through his remarkable talent and good old-fashioned American work ethic. By all rights, John Wayne should have been living in a palace filled with enough treasures and luxuries to make a sultan blush. But instead of dwelling among the world's biggest stars in Hollywood, John Wayne decided the place for him and his family was the seaside community of Newport Beach, California. Duke grew up among the poverty of the Great Depression and, like most Americans of his generation, knew the greatest riches this world could offer were a warm and loving home. The community of 36,000 provided the perfect nest for him, Pilar and their children to live out their American Dream.

From their modest waterside home on Bayshore Drive, the Waynes shared meals, memories and holidays together. Duke's youngest son Ethan recalls the smell of bacon and eggs in the morning signaling that his famous father was already tucking into his breakfast. "He'd have a plate of eggs and a separate plate just piled with crispy bacon," Ethan says. "He'd open a can of green chili salsa and dump it over the top— the whole can on top of the bacon, and that's how he'd eat it." When John Wayne wanted to give Pilar a break from cooking and treat the family to a meal out on the town, the celebrity didn't shy away from his adoring

public. Duke could often be found at local eateries such as A Restaurant and the Galley Cafe, where he would order a chili burger big enough to satisfy the hearty appetite he had built up over a day's work. Residents of Newport grew accustomed to seeing the actor tool around town in his modest station wagon, whether he was dropping the kids off at school or just running down to the grocery store to help out with errands. "A lot of times he'd pick me up from school," says

Duke enjoys a meal with his wife, Pilar, and their three kids, Ethan, Marisa and Aissa, 1969.

Marisa, his youngest child. "We could walk around town and go to Sears." And of course, anyone searching for the legend would first stop by the Balboa Bay Club, a social establishment frequented by both locals and out-of-town luminaries such as Humphrey Bogart and Lauren Bacall. Duke could often be found there sharing a drink and a laugh with a friend or three. Thanks to the love, peace and privacy given to him by Newport, he was a man who had a lot to smile about.

DUKE...KNEW THE GREATEST RICHES THIS WORLD COULD OFFER WERE A WARM AND LOVING HOME.

Duke's celebrity status didn't keep his kids from living a (mostly) typical life in Newport Beach. "There weren't paparazzi. We didn't have bodyguards," recalled Ethan in the *Orange County Register* in 2011.

Duke holds up his son Ethan on the *Wild Goose*. John Wayne's children would sleep in bunk beds in a cabin on the boat.

Home on the Water

Determined to see his family enjoy as much of America's bounty and shining seas as he could, John Wayne didn't settle for spending afternoons cooped up indoors—after all, why play chess in the living room when you could be seeing the world at the same time? And so the Wayne family often took to the water to spend time together, on one of Duke's most prized possessions—the *Wild Goose*. This 136-foot former World War II Navy minesweeper wasn't just some idle toy purchased by Duke to cross "own a boat" off his bucket list. It was a haven for him and his family away from the ever-present pressures of managing the biggest career in Hollywood, a place where he felt most like himself. "He was just so happy, just to be able to relax," Ethan told the *Los Angeles Times*. "He had to [manage] so much in town, it was his place [to relax]."

John Wayne always had a special affinity for the ocean and life on the shore. As a teenager, he would spend hours bodysurfing in the Pacific with friends. It's no coincidence that when Duke became wealthy enough to live wherever his heart desired, he decided to settle his family in Newport Beach, California, where the hush of the ocean's waves constantly murmured (the Newport Beach City Council has since enshrined their town's love for the legend by declaring May 26—Duke's birthday—as John Wayne Day).

In 1962, Duke became the owner of the *Wild Goose*, which would carry him and his friends and family into countless good times. Bert Minshall, the former captain of the *Wild Goose*, recalls the laughter started with his first meeting with the actor. "One day after Duke joined us on the boat, I was introduced to John Wayne. I saw him eyeing my new deck shoes, and all of sudden he spits at my shoes," Minshall says. "I was too quick and pulled my feet away so the spit landed on the rug. Duke is laughing and puts his big hand on my shoulder and says 'Always spit on new shoes for good luck.'"

Minshall's first meeting with Duke encapsulated everything the icon strived to make life on board the *Wild Goose* about—a fun and relaxing refuge separate from the rest of the world, where the only concerns should be where the next good time would come from. For Duke, that usually was in the boat's main salon, where he would idle away the hours playing cards or chess with whomever happened to be around. "It was always bridge, or backgammon or chess," Minshall says. "He was a good chess player." Visitors might also have found John Wayne relaxing with a book, absorbed in one of the accounts of history he loved. It was a passion he took pride in, even going so far as to decorate the salon with scenes of fleets clashing in battle from centuries past. "There was an illustration from a book on old sea battles Duke had blown up and put on the bulkhead," Minshall

Duke on board the *Wild Goose*, his home away from home. On trips to the frigid waters by Alaska, Duke would sometimes chip ice off glaciers to use in cooling down his drinks.

JOHN WAYNE ALWAYS HAD A SPECIAL AFFINITY FOR THE OCEAN AND LIFE ON THE SHORE.

says. "It was about two, three feet tall and covered the width of the salon—about 15 feet." Of course, Duke knew real relaxation isn't just lounging around like a bump on a log—it's also about seizing the day. An avid fisherman, John Wayne and family would often plot the *Wild Goose* to his favorite spots to cast a line, whether in Mexico or in Canada. "In the morning, around 9 a.m., he'd go out there with professional guides, and come back with 30, 35 pounds of salmon," Minshall says.

Duke may no longer be with us, but the *Wild Goose* is still around, having passed into the possession of Hornblower Cruises, who welcomes anyone hankering to climb aboard an important piece of the legend's personal history. Visitors to the boat's home at Newport Harbor can see the bulkheads that witnessed thousands of jokes, card games and good meals with friends and family—all the moments that constituted Duke's fondest memories.

Duke and Ethan enjoy themselves on the log ride at Knott's Berry Farm. Always a fan of the park, John Wayne once sent cases of their strawberry preserves to American servicemen in Vietnam.

From left: Jacquetta LeForce, Duke and son Patrick take a look at a calf; the actor talking with some cowboys outside 26 Bar Ranch. Besides Duke and Louis Johnson, Ken Reafsnyder of Knott's Berry Farm also had a stake in the ranch.

Back at the Ranch

Duke made his fame and fortune by telling the stories of men who spent their days ranging the ranches. He may have been the biggest star in Hollywood, but his past and personality gave him an affinity for life on the open range, and it was this passion that led him to Eagar, Arizona, and the 26 Bar Ranch. Not only was the cattle ranch one of Duke's most successful investments, it was also one of his favorites. "He definitely had a love of and an affinity for this ranch—there's no question about that," explains Michael Goldman, author of *John Wayne: The Genuine Article.*

During the '60s and '70s, 26 Bar Ranch's 17,000 acres played host to some of America's finest Hereford cattle, and Louis Johnson and John Wayne were at the heart of it all. Putting John Wayne on a cattle ranch seems obvious, and, according to Goldman, it was

Duke's familiarity with the cowboy life that made ranching such an attractive proposition. "He was already well acquainted with riding and roping and things like that," Goldman says. "Because of what he did for a living, he knew cowboys and stunt men and people who performed in rodeos. Those were largely the people with whom he worked to train and learn his Western persona early in his career. The ranch was a venture that went very well because he had a great partner and because he had a real interest in this particular type of business, as opposed to something else that might have been just for an investment."

"Right up until his death, he got into numerous outside businesses of all sorts, shapes and flavors," continues Goldman. "There were things like diamond mines, there were some oil wells. There were shrimp boats." All of Duke's business endeavors required partners because he spent so much of his time tirelessly working on movies.

John Wayne found his best business partner yet in Arizona rancher Louis Johnson. Johnson would manage Duke's Arizona holdings until the actor's death in 1979. By then, Duke's cattle ranching enterprises alone would be worth millions. "He eventually became so close to Louis Johnson that Johnson was actually one of the executors of his entire estate," notes Goldman.

But the real value of the ranch came from the memories Duke made there with his family. They would frequently congregate at the ranch every Thanksgiving for big feasts planned around steer auctions and other events hosted by John Wayne. "Patrick Wayne would often work there in the summers, and other family members were frequent visitors," says Goldman. For a couple of days a year, at least, the Waynes were home on the range.

John Wayne surveys a ranch, which he partially owns, c. 1969. For a stretch of 28 miles, Arizona State Highway 347 is known as John Wayne Parkway.

Duke shakes the hand of an American soldier in Vietnam. As the actor told *Stars and Stripes*, "If nothing else, [my visit] gave the kids something else to write home about."

★ 1967–1973 ★
PROUD PATRIOT

AS THE 1960s drew to a close, it became apparent to almost everyone that the decade would go down in history books as one of America's most tumultuous. The Greatest Generation began to make room in the hall of power for young Americans who only knew the peace and prosperity earned by their elders, and social norms that once seemed set in stone were swept aside. The Civil Rights movement continued to fight for the rights of African-American and minority citizens, calling attention to the injustices they suffered with such force that even the most apathetic American was forced to confront the strain of white supremacy infecting the country. Women also continued questioning the unspoken rules governing how they should act (and what they could do with their own bodies) with increased vigor and incredulity, and Americans of all creeds and color started casting a more-than skeptical eye toward authority in all of its forms.

While this sweeping social change brought hope and dignity to millions of

The March on the Pentagon, October 21, 1967. Nearly 700 protesters were arrested on charges of civil disobedience.

American citizens, it wasn't without a price, sometimes one paid in blood. On April 4, 1968, Civil Rights leader Martin Luther King Jr. fell to an assassin's bullet in Memphis, Tennessee, sparking mass race riots in New York, Washington, D.C., Chicago and nearly every other major city in the country. The carnage would continue that June with the fatal shooting of Bobby Kennedy, a sitting senator and presidential hopeful who embodied to many young Americans the winds of change sweeping the country. The brutal police beatings of enraged leftist protesters outside of the Democratic National Convention in Chicago seemed to cap off a summer of domestic turmoil for Americans, who were growing used to the nightly news resembling footage from a war movie.

Of course, an actual war was still being waged by American soldiers thousands of miles away in the jungles of Southeast Asia. The Vietnam War had escalated to the point where tens of thousands of young men had lost life and limb in a country few Americans could identify on a map, for reasons that seemed increasingly opaque. When the Viet Cong launched the Tet Offensive in the beginning of 1968, a massive coordinated attack on supposedly safe strongholds in the American-allied South, the government's assertions that the United States was close to victory were revealed as naive at best and dishonest at worst.

The desire of many Americans to end the Vietnam War played a major role in the election of Richard Nixon (a friend of Duke's and a fellow Californian) in 1968, as the Republican candidate promised to extricate

American forces while retaining the country's honor. It took Nixon more than four years to make good on his promise to end hostilities between North Vietnam and the United States, and only after first expanding the war to Cambodia and Laos. After America ceased hostilities in January 1973, an exhausted South Vietnam continued the war until the capture of its capital, Saigon, in April 1975.

As America transformed both at home and abroad, one comforting constant was John Wayne and his unabashed patriotism. At a time when expressing a love for the Red, White and Blue struck many as corny or old-fashioned, Duke's eloquence and authenticity helped rally like-minded Americans around the idea that the United States was a force of good in the world. For the soldiers in Vietnam (and the public who still believed in their mission), Duke made 1968's *The Green Berets*, a war movie celebrating the exploits of the U.S. Army's Special Forces operating in Southeast Asia. Although many critics took umbrage with the film's unabashedly pro-war tone, Duke didn't mind that he triggered a handful of men and women paid to write about movies so long as he was telling the story he felt the country needed to hear. "*The Green Berets* would have been successful regardless of what the critics did," Duke said in an interview. "But it might have taken the public longer to find out about the picture if they hadn't made so much noise about it."

John Wayne continued to promote a pure love of country, liberal critics be damned, with patriotic television specials such as *Swing Out, Sweet Land* extolling the virtues of the American experience—a necessary reminder in the midst of the chaos of the times.

President Nixon at a Vietnam War Press Conference, 1970. Nixon assured citizens the U.S. forces would soon withdraw from Cambodia.

Maj. Gen. John M. Wright and John Wayne at Fort Benning, Georgia. Wright, who was commander at Fort Benning at the time of the film's production, granted Duke permission to film at his base because he believed the movie would bolster the military's image. Opposite: A poster for *The Green Berets*.

The Green Berets

Throughout his five-decade career (and beyond), John Wayne reigned as one of Hollywood's most popular stars. One of the reasons people welcomed Duke into their hearts was because of the man's pure authenticity. He always stood up for the principles he believed were right and just, and his unwavering ideals made him a role model for generations of Americans looking for a hero. Duke's steadfast faith in life, liberty and the pursuit of happiness became especially clear during the latter half of the 1960s, as wave after wave of change rocked the nation at every level—art, entertainment, politics and more. Even the support of Americans for their soldiers fighting in distant lands came under fire, a shock for those who remembered the lockstep unity characterizing the home front during World War II. John Wayne wanted to show America's fighting men and women thousands of miles from home that the nation's biggest celebrity hadn't forgotten their valor and sacrifice, and he did so in the way he knew best—by making a movie, one still fondly watched today.

Similar to *The Alamo* (1960), *The Green Berets* (1968) saw Duke intimately involved in every aspect of the film's creation, from producing to directing to acting. And though the movie lacks the grandeur of the passion project Duke spent a decade creating, *The Green Berets* is every bit as ambitious and heartfelt in its message to the American people.

John Wayne based the story of *The Green Berets* on the 1965 book of the same name by Robin Moore, and like its source material, the movie follows the exploits of a unit of the U.S. Army Special Forces (nicknamed "The Green Berets" thanks to their distinctive headgear) operating in South Vietnam. Drawing perhaps from his experience in *Sands of Iwo Jima*, John Wayne sought the cooperation of the United States government in making the movie a realistic depiction of the war. To that end, Duke (with the blessings of Uncle Sam) journeyed to the frontlines of Vietnam himself in 1966 to visit several bases and gather a sense of the struggles facing the men battling communism in the jungles and rice paddies of the war-torn country. The Department of Defense also reviewed the film's script for accuracy and helped provide technical assistance to make the final product as authentic as possible.

Fidelity to the look of the conflict was just one of the matters weighing on Duke's mind during filming. More than any other film since *The Alamo*, John Wayne wanted to send a message to the American people, and similar to the Texan war epic, *The Green Berets* wears its heart on its sleeve. "It was an

American film about American boys who were heroes over there," Duke said in a 1971 interview. The protagonists, Col. Mike Kirby (John Wayne) and his band of Green Berets (including a soldier played by a young George Takei) are all stalwart examples of American bravery and honor, working hand-in-hand with their South Vietnamese allies to liberate the country from the nefarious communists based in the North. David Janssen plays a skeptical journalist embedded with the unit, giving voice to the millions of Americans back home who in varying degrees doubted the righteousness of the military's mission in Southeast Asia. By the end of the film, the cruelty of the North Vietnamese combined

with the valor of the Green Berets convinces him America is doing the right thing, a conversion Duke hoped would be replicated a million times over once audiences understood the true scope of the war.

As expected, the liberal-leaning critics didn't look kindly on a film with old-fashioned patriotic sensibilities. But a quiet majority of everyday Americans seemed to have been longing for a movie celebrating the country rather than pointing out its flaws. *The Green Berets* was a financial success, earning $21 million on a $7 million budget, and continues to be one of the most historically important movies in John Wayne's filmography, an ode to the American values that made him a star.

Western Costume Co.
HOLLYWOOD
NO. 2066-1
NAME John Wayne
CHEST 48 SLEEVE 19

Clockwise from top left: Duke leads a charge in a scene from the movie. The star also directed much of the film, sharing that duty with fellow Iowa-native Ray Kellogg; from the John Wayne Archive, fatigues worn by Duke in *The Green Berets* with a tag displaying his measurements for one garment as "chest 48, sleeve 19"; a beret Duke wore in the film.

From the John Wayne Archive, a collection of Duke's memorabilia from *The Green Berets* (1968) consisting of (from left) the beret he wore for the film lying on top of his scripts; his personal copy of the book, authored by Robin Moore in 1965. Moore also co-authored the lyrics to the hit 1966 song "Ballad of the Green Berets," an instrumental version of which is featured in the 1968 movie; a statuette given to John Wayne by the real-life Green Berets.

Some of the most popular entertainers of the 1970s pitched in to give America her due, including (outside clockwise from top left): Ann-Margret; Bob Hope; Jack Benny; Lucille Ball; William Shatner; Michael Landon; Roscoe Lee Browne; Lorne Greene; Phyllis Diller; Bing Crosby and Johnny Cash. John Wayne (pictured center) and Ed McMahon (directly below) also participated, along with many other celebrities.

Singing Her Praises

Featuring a who's who of '70s entertainment, John Wayne's Emmy-winning and first televised special set a high bar. Originally titled *Swing Out, Sweet Land* and broadcast on NBC on November 29, 1970, *John Wayne's Tribute to America* included stars Lucille Ball, Jack Benny, Johnny Cash, Bing Crosby, Bob Hope, Ann-Margret, Dean Martin, William Shatner, Red Skelton, Tom Smothers and many others parodying important players throughout American history, as well as just being their talented selves.

The 80-minute special was initially rooted in politics, poised as John Wayne's personal response to growing protest against the war in Vietnam. Three years after the anti-war movement brought about in the "Summer of Love," the country stood greatly divided, and this was Duke's attempt to lead America back to a patriotic place that supported its troops and relished its greatness. Despite its political origins, John Wayne and company managed to keep the program lighthearted, entertaining and upbeat. The consummate conservative—who served as host and narrator of the special—even poked a bit of fun at himself, promising during the show's introduction that it would be "short on preaching." He continued, "Countries are like people, some take themselves so seriously that you won't get a laugh out of them in 100 years. And others are more apt than not to stick their tongues in their cheek and tell funny stories about themselves. And America, thank God, is one of those yarn-spinning places."

The special used laughter, music and celebrities to boost morale and in turn received its fair share of accolades, including an Emmy for director Dominic Frontiere for Outstanding Achievement in Musical Direction. *Tribute* was certainly not lacking in lessons, however, as John Wayne led viewers through important moments of America's history with his famous pals along to help illustrate the past with a kick of humor. In the first sketch, Michael Landon portrays Peter Minuit buying Manhattan Island from a Native American (*Bonanza* costar Dan Blocker); Jack Benny plays a citizen asking George Washington (Lorne Greene) about that silver dollar he supposedly skipped across the Potomac River; Lucille Ball depicts Miss Liberty; Bob Hope and Ann-Margret entertain the troops at Valley Forge; Bing Crosby plays Mark Twain alongside freed slave Frederick Douglass (Roscoe Lee Browne); and Dean Martin is shown as inventor Eli Whitney—to name just a few of Duke's famous friends who appear in the multitude of tongue-in-cheek sketches.

There were also musical numbers by Johnny Cash, Glen Campbell, Leslie Uggams and the entire cast who unsurprisingly belted out "God Bless America." The program, a hit at the time with Duke's fans and still widely available on DVD today, proved patriotism was in fact still alive and well. The man put it best in his introduction to the show: "What I'm trying to say is that some folks have the idea that patriotism has gone out of fashion." But not if Duke had anything to say about it.

Dear Mr. President

Despite periodic pleas that he run for office himself, John Wayne repeatedly shrugged at the notion, declaring in a 1967 telegram, "As the saying goes, I'd rather be right than president." While uninterested in occupying it himself, John Wayne wasn't shy about giving advice to whomever held the Oval Office. Duke's presidential correspondence started after he campaigned for President Dwight D. Eisenhower and was invited to speak at Ike's inauguration festivities in 1953. Soon after, John Wayne began corresponding with then-Vice President Richard Nixon, and they eventually struck up a friendship. After Nixon took the White House in 1968, a flurry of correspondence sealed the duo's flourishing bond. At one point, Duke sent Nixon a letter suggesting the actor would run for president and warned Nixon to "look out." Nixon quickly wrote back, claiming, "Duke is a better title than President!"

John Wayne also sent Democrats JFK, LBJ and Jimmy Carter telegrams after they defeated his preferred Republican candidates, reminding them he was an American first and a partisan second. "Congratulations, sir, from one of the loyal opposition," he wrote to all three Democratic victors. Upon receiving his letter from Duke, Carter invited him to participate in the inauguration festivities, and the screen legend graciously accepted. From that point onward, a curious correspondence developed between the two men, despite their political differences, with Duke periodically sending Carter notes politely criticizing his policies. When the actor passed away in 1979, President Carter eulogized him to the nation, stating, "John Wayne was bigger than life...He was a symbol of so many of the qualities that make America great." It was a bipartisan vote of approval for Duke's all-American character.

2-023848E308002 11/03/76 ICS IPMRNCZ CSP LSAB
1 7146469740 MGM TDRN NEWPORT BEACH CA 11-03 1226P EST

Pres Carter file

BATJAC PRODUCTIONS PS
9570 WILSHIRE BLVD SUITE 400
BEVERLY HILLS CA 90212

THIS MAILGRAM IS A CONFIRMATION COPY OF THE FOLLOWING MESSAGE:

7146469740 TDRN NEWPORT BEACH CA 8 11-03 1226P EST
PMS PRESIDENT ELECT JIMMY CARTER
100 COLONY SQ
ATLANTA GA 30361
CONGRATULATIONS SIR FROM ONE OF THE LOYAL OPPOSITION
    JOHN WAYNE

12:26 EST

MGMCOMP MGM

JIMMY CARTER

November 10, 1976

To John Wayne

Your congratulations are indeed appreciated!

I trust the only area in which we will find our-
selves in opposition is that of Party loyalty.
I will need your help in the coming years, and
hope to have your support.

Sincerely,

Jimmy

Jimmy Carter

JC/sc

★ DUKE'S telegram
congratulating Jimmy
Carter on his victorious
campaign for president
and Carter's response.
Although a devout
Republican, Duke
always put country
ahead of politics and
gave the commander in
chief his due regardless
of party. ★

The Honorable Richard M. Nixon
November 23, 1971
Page 2

You may think me very presumptuous. I hope you do not, but
I would feel negligent in my duty as an American if I did not
make this request as a sincere friend, or at least acquain-
tance -- we have had a martini or two together.

                              Respectfully,

                              John Wayne

JW:ms

219P PDT AUG 1 72 LA288 CTA328
CT JAB055 TC PDF PARIS TENN 1 233P CDT
JOHN WAYNE CARE OF MARY ST JOHN SERVICE
5451 MARTHAN ST LOSA
I FOR ONE A CHARTER MEMBER OF THE AMERICAN PARTY WOULD LIKE
FOR YOU TO CONSIDER BEING ELECTED TO THE PRESIDENT OF USA ON
THE AMERICAN PARTY
ELLIOTT E MOODY PARIS TENN.

JOHN WAYNE
August 1, 1972

SF-1201 (R5-69)

Dear Mr. President:

Look out!

Watch your Ps and Qs!

[signature: Duke]

THE WHITE HOUSE
WASHINGTON

August 3, 1972

AUG 14 1972

★ CLOCKWISE
FROM LEFT:
John Wayne invites
President Nixon
for a drink via
the post; despite
encouragement
from fans and fellow
patriots, Duke never
ran for president,
but he joked with
the nation's highest
in command that he
had the option, as
seen in this light-
hearted exchange;
Duke shares a laugh
with Nixon. ★

Dear Duke:

Don't do it. After all Duke is a

better title than President!

Sincerely,

[signature]

Mr. John Wayne
Suite 332
9071 Wilshire Boulevard
Beverly Hills, California 90211

STATEMENT BY JOHN WAYNE

You are asking that question because of the news impact of a recent statement in a national magazine. I am going to answer it to the best of my ability -- not as an actor, but because of my right as a plain American citizen.

I think the first requisite of our next President is that he be a God-fearing man -- not necessarily a scholar of deep religious subjects -- but as in the sense of Abraham Lincoln, who, because he was not a regular church-goer to any particular denomination, was once asked his views on religion and if he had ever prayed. He answered: "Yes. I have been driven to my knees many times by the overwhelming fact that I had no other place to go."

Secondly, history repeats itself. It has been said a thousand times, but we seem to overlook it. Franklin Delano Roosevelt, Harry Truman, and Dwight Eisenhower had the same problems to face that the men in the Alamo, Houston, Washington, and Lincoln had to face -- perhaps a little more complex, but basically the same problems. We hope that "The Alamo" will cue people into realizing that the leaders of that day faced up to their problems immediately and head-on. They did not complacently sit by and allow the monster to build for the next generation.

I think the next President should be a man who would emulate General Sam Houston, who said: "I live by the political axiom of always meeting issues head-on and at once, rather than leave my children the dread legacy of their father's indecision."

It is obvious that most of our internal as well as international problems are caused by one thing: Communism. Not the Russian people or the Chinese people - but Communism.

Since this is obvious, I want a leader that will confront this issue, even if it is unpalatable and frightening to the people -- a leader who will make it uncompromisingly clear that we will fight if that's what the enemy forces on us; but that come hell or high water, we will not again retreat in front of Kremlin bullying. If as a nation we do not show some moral guts, we will lose our strength and purpose as a member of the world community.

My feeling is that our political parties are more interested in votes than in principle. They are smoke-screening the menace to our very existence by political generalities and traditional cure-alls, and are avoiding the main issue. Whether we have more Democrats than Republicans, or vice

versa -- whether Oregon has six-lane highways before Oklahoma does -- is not important at the moment. But whether there is a small footpath for Communism to the minds of our children is of the utmost importance. If we are moral and spiritual cowards, they will have no respect for our way of life.

Therefore, to lead my country I want a man who will take the offensive against our common enemy -- who will make the people face up to the possibility of war. I want a man who will raise a banner saying: "Fear God, but not Communism."

I want a man who will re-establish by thought and deed the United States of America as a bulwark of freedom and justice -- a man who will make America's principles and attitude so strong that other Western and Eastern countries and people all over the world can unite with us to prove the truth of the latest Chinese proverb: "There can be no peaceful co-existence with Communism."

The history of the past twenty-five years proves the unpleasant fact that if a determined unity is not developed in the free world, it will go out of existence.

I think that the American people are willing and anxious to find a man who will insure this kind of leadership.

5451 Marathon Street
Hollywood, Calif. 90038
November 23, 1971

The Honorable Richard M. Nixon
The White House
Washington, D. C.

Dear Mr. President:

Congratulations on your stand on Amchitka.

Quite obviously your time is valuable. I hate to burden you
with anything but, as you know, although I am not a politician
I have taken a firm stand for you because of my confidence
in you as a clear-thinking leader.

Although logic demands some dialogue with Mao, in spite of
200 million victims and a trillion American dollars, and in
spite of much dialogue and bridge building, the attitude of
the Communists has been unswerving; so I'll have to admit
it was quite a shocker when I heard you were going to Red
China and throw Taiwan to the jackals in the United Nations.
Everyone knew that Red China would not accept that seat
unless Taiwan was discarded. All foreign newspapers have
been stating that that was part of Mao's ultimatum for a Com-
munist-Chinese acceptance of a seat in the United Nations.

With all the hysteria about getting the boys out of Vietnam, I
found what I think is a worthwhile article in Reader's Digest,
in explaining to any Doves who would listen, why and how we
were in Vietnam and the reasonableness of same.

So, the favor I would most respectfully request is that in
your spare time you read the Reader's Digest article and
the articles accompanying it. I am sure there are a great
number of Americans who reflect on our government's present attitude as does Mr. Putnam in his article.

You may think me very presumptuous. I hope you do not, but
I would feel negligent in my duty as an American if I did not
make this request as a sincere friend, or at least acquain-
tance -- we have had a martini or two together.

                              Respectfully,

                              John Wayne

JW:ms

THE WHITE HOUSE

WASHINGTON

January 13, 1972

Dear Duke:

While this note is belated, I did want to thank
you for your letter of November 23 and its en-
closures. Obviously, a very large number of
Americans - myself included - were disturbed
by the expulsion of the Republic of China from
the United Nations. However, let me assure
you that my decision to travel to Peking was in
no way connected with the United Nation's action
as far as this Administration is concerned.

We repeatedly emphasized to every member state
of the UN that the pros and cons regarding the
admission of the People's Republic of China had
absolutely no bearing on the right of Taiwan to
its seat in the General Assembly. We worked
very hard over a long period of time to persuade
the UN members not to expel the Republic of
China. Unfortunately, we just did not have the
votes to win our case, and I think most dispas-
sionate observers of the United Nations share
our feeling that the expulsion of Taiwan only
serves to weaken that world body.

You have pointed out in your letter that logic
demands some dialogue with the People's Republic
of China. I agree, and that is why I am willing to
take the first step. Clearly the generation of peace
we all seek cannot be established while the People's

★ JOHN WAYNE often
sent presidents articles from
magazines and newspapers
that raised salient policy
questions, usually with his
own commentary attached.
From left: A letter in which
Duke asks Nixon about
his foreign policy, an area
the president considered
his forte; Nixon's lengthy
and thoughtful reply,
underscoring that Duke was
more than able to hold his
own with the nation's highest
political authorities. ★

-2-

Republic is excluded from the mainstream of
world affairs, including contact with the United
States. But we have no intention of abandoning
our commitments to Taiwan, and we have made
this fact well-known to everyone concerned. We
are determined to stand by our friends, just as
we have stood by the South Vietnamese.

I hope this will allay some of your fears and
perhaps clear the air. Needless to say, I always welcome receiving your comments, and
I hope you will feel free in the months ahead to
give me the benefit of your views and counsel.

With warm personal regards,

Sincerely,

Duke meets with President Nixon and Henry Kissinger, who was then Nixon's National Security Advisor, July 1972. Just a month prior to this meeting, five men broke into the Democratic National Committee's headquarters in the Watergate office complex, beginning a scandal that would bring down the Nixon presidency.

America, Why I Love Her

In 1973, troubled times brought on by the Watergate Scandal and the Vietnam War inspired Duke to record a sonic love letter to America. Americans of multiple generations had grown up with Duke's comforting, familiar image on the screen, but the Hollywood star decided to turn to another medium to spread his patriotic sentiments to the people—music. Partnering with writer and character actor John Mitchum (the younger brother of Robert), John Wayne recorded a 10-track record entitled *America, Why I Love Her*, on which he recited stirring odes to our country's might and majesty over a background of instrumentals. The title track was a poem (seen to the right) praising our great nation's beauty and outstanding citizenry, from the shores of the Atlantic to the beaches of the Pacific. The record also includes "The Pledge of Allegiance" and other pieces extolling the bravery and sacrifice Americans have made throughout history to preserve the land of the free. It was a hit upon its release, garnering a Grammy nomination for Best Spoken Word Album in 1974. And Americans continue to turn to the record, especially during trying times. After the September 11 terrorist attacks, citizens leaned on Duke's strength once again, finding comfort in his voice and his boundless love for America when John Wayne's family re-released the patriotic album.

You ask me Why I Love Her? Well, give me time and I'll explain.

Have you seen a Kansas sunset or an Arizona rain?

Have you drifted on a bayou down Louisiana way?

Have you watched a cold fog drifting over San Francisco Bay?

Have you heard a bobwhite calling in the Carolina pines,

Or heard the bellow of a diesel at the Appalachia mines?

Does the call of Niagara thrill you when you hear her waters roar?

Do you look with awe and wonder at her Massachusetts shore,

Where men who braved a hard new world first stepped on Plymouth's rock?

And do you think of them when you stroll along a New York City dock?

Have you seen a snowflake drifting in the Rockies, way up high?

Have you seen the sun come blazing down from a bright Nevada sky?

Do you hail to the Columbia as she rushes to the sea,

Or bow your head at Gettysburg at our struggle to be free?

Have you seen the mighty Tetons? Have you watched an eagle soar?

Have you seen the Mississippi roll along Missouri's shore?

Have you felt a chill at Michigan when on a winter's day

Her waters rage along the shore in thunderous display?

Does the word "Aloha" make you warm? Do you stare in disbelief

When you see the surf come roaring in at Waimea Reef?

From Alaska's cold to the Everglades, from the Rio Grande to Maine,

My heart cries out, my pulse runs fast at the might of her domain.

You ask me Why I Love Her? I've a million reasons why:

My Beautiful America, beneath God's wide, wide sky.

JOHN WAYNE

FOLKS:

All of my life I've felt privileged to have had good friends around me, privileged to have been able to do the kind of work I know and love the best, and to have been born in a country whose immense beauty and grandeur are matched only by the greatness of her people.

For a number of years I have tried to express a deep and profound love for these things; to be able to say what I feel in my heart. And, now, in this album, I've had the chance to do so.

I know most of you feel the same as I do about our country. Now and then we gripe about some of her imperfections, but sometimes that's good. Especially if it gets us working together to make things better. It seems to me we often take too much for granted, and have a tendency to forget "The Good Things About America."

My hope and prayer is that everyone know and love our country for what she really is and what she stands for. May we nurture her strengths and strengthen her weaknesses so that she will always be a "Land Of The Free, and Home Of The Brave."

Sincerely,

John Wayne
John Wayne

RCA
LSP-4828 STEREO

Side 1
Why I Love Her (2:14)
The Hyphen (2:29)
Mis Raices Estan Aqui *(My Roots Are Buried Here)* (2:41)
The People (3:40)
An American Boy Grows Up (4:29)

Side 2
Face the Flag (3:53)
The Good Things (2:40)
The Pledge of Allegiance *(BMI/ASCAP 4:19)*
Why Are You Marching, Son? (3:58)
Taps (2:01)

Entire selections publisher—ASCAP, except as noted.
Produced by Billy Liebert for Bertell Productions, Inc.
Arranged and Conducted by Billy Liebert

JOHN WAYNE
AMERICA,
WHY I LOVE HER

John Wayne

★ AMERICA, *Why I Love Her*, Duke's spoken word album, released in 1973, from the John Wayne Archive. The album spent 13 weeks on *Billboard* charts. ★

An Evolving Legend

As the eldest child in a family who moved from town to town attempting to make ends meet, Duke learned the importance of adapting to shifting circumstances at a young age. While steadfast in his authenticity as an American legend, John Wayne didn't oppose change so long as it made sense and was for the better. Nothing better sums up his attitude than the words on his gravestone in Corona del Mar, California, which read, "Tomorrow is the most important thing in life. Comes into us at midnight very clean. It's perfect when it arrives and it puts itself in our hands. It hopes we've learned something from yesterday." Duke, an actor whose filmography includes both silent movies and 3-D films, always looked forward to the future while retaining the wisdom of the past, an attitude that helped him mature his on-screen image from youthful loner to the older gunslinger who has seen it all and is ready to impart his wisdom on the next generation.

Duke began his seamless transition into an elder statesmen of the silver screen in 1969, with his portrayal of Rooster Cogburn in *True Grit*. Rather than deny the passage of time, John Wayne set aside the image of the handsome Western hero in favor of the flawed, weathered, one-eyed marshal. And the transition didn't go unnoticed by audiences: "Wayne is now like a stoic grandfather in the saddle," writes Alexander Walker in his 1970 book *Stardom: The Hollywood Phenomenon*. "But the same self-reliance is there: And he has stood so long in the dwindling forest of American screen heroes that his seasoned eminence is undeniably splendid." The Academy also noticed Duke's fresh portrayal of Rooster Cogburn, awarding him an Oscar for Best Actor in 1970.

Just a year after receiving the honor, the actor was making the most of his later years again, this time as the titular character in *Big Jake*. At a time when the landscape of Tinseltown was appearing barren to some critics, Duke's resonance as the rugged old Jacob "Big Jake" McCandles stood out. In the July 1, 1971, edition of *The Village Voice*, Michael Kerbel wrote: "If one loves John Wayne—as I do—the film can be quite moving. After all, Hollywood and the star system are dying, but there he is, after 40 years, still attracting audiences, still infusing each scene with his legendary personality."

And that legendary personality—forged by a lifetime of experiences both on and off the screen—would have a particularly profound effect in 1972's *The Cowboys*. As Wil Andersen, a seasoned cattleman forced to hire young schoolboys as replacement ranchers, Duke brought a tender touch to the character likely inspired by his greatest role offscreen. "Wayne is, of course, marvelously indestructible, and he has become an almost perfect father figure," said *The New York Times* following the film's release. But it would be Archer Winston of the *New York Post* who would summarize the actor's adaptability with a sentiment befitting the legend, writing, "John Wayne again shows that he's like vintage wine—the older he gets, the better."

John Wayne and Norman Howell in a scene from *The Cowboys* (1972). The film features one of the few times John Wayne's character dies on-screen. In this case, he is shot in the back by a villain played by Bruce Dern.

John Wayne on the set of *The Shootist* (1976). Footage from *Hondo* (1953), *Rio Bravo* (1959) and *El Dorado* (1967) was included after the beginning credits to introduce Duke's character, J.B. Books.

★ 1973–1979 ★
ELDER STATESMAN

AS THE repercussions of the 1960s' tendency toward excess were felt across the country, there were more than a few Americans of what would later be called the "Greatest Generation," who felt their beloved country was going proverbially south. According to Uniform Crime Reports from the Federal Bureau of Investigation, the second half of the 1960s marked the beginning of an almost 30-year increase of criminal activity in the United States, with crime rates doubling across the board between 1960 and 1970. Before long, the neverending torrent of criminal stories would even affect the White House itself.

Clint Eastwood in *Dirty Harry* (1971).

In 1960, for every 100,000 people, there were approximately 160 violent crimes, 60 robberies and 500 burglaries. In 1970, those numbers had jumped to 360 violent crimes, 170 robberies and almost 1,100 burglaries. Crime rates continued on an upward tick until the mid-1990s, at which point they leveled off and began decreasing again—though today, crime rates are still not quite as low as they were 60 years ago. As the United States collectively became more wary, filmmakers were inspired to create new, modern detective films like *Dirty Harry* (1971) and *The French Connection* (1971). John Wayne even got in on the action, making two underrated detective films in the '70s, *McQ* (1974) and *Brannigan* (1975).

While most Americans were still relatively safe—360 violent crimes per 100,000 people meant less than 1 percent of the population was affected—the perception that the country had become a considerably more dangerous place was palpable. News of serial killers, including Ed Kemper and the Zodiac Killer, swept the nation. Much of pop culture centered on New York City, which was notoriously dangerous in the 1970s (the murder rate more than tripled between 1963 and 1972, and by 1979, there were more than 250 felonies each week in the subway system).

For conservative Americans, a group with which John Wayne always identified, the dramatic cultural changes that saw the straight-laced 1950s give way to the experimentation and freedom of the 1960s were cataclysmic. Issues that had seemed to be black and white during the Eisenhower years had slowly but surely slipped into grayscale by the time Gerald Ford was inaugurated. The liberal/conservative divide broken open in 1968 remained as wide as it had been in generations, exemplified by the televised debates between William F. Buckley and Gore Vidal that pitted new-style liberalism against tight-fisted conservatism. John Wayne was acutely aware of this divide and bridged it through parody when he accepted an award from Harvard's Hasty Pudding Club, arriving at Cambridge in a tank.

It was this sort of gameness that defined the ways in which conservatives like Duke reacted to the more liberal society in which they found themselves. Remaining ever optimistic about American values and their future, and still loyal to the GOP, these new conservatives would nonetheless embrace across-the-aisle fraternization and common-sense approaches to modern questions. By the time this sort of ethos won the White House with George W. Bush's "compassionate conservatism," Duke

Duke campaigns alongside President Gerald Ford, 1976. Though Ford lost the reelection, he and Duke remained friends until the film star's death.

was gone. But his reaction to the liberal Jimmy Carter's election as president in 1976 exemplifies its essence. After his win, Carter received a telegram from Duke, a member of "the loyal opposition," congratulating him.

Carter had just ousted Gerald Ford, a close personal friend of Duke's, but the actor harbored no bitterness once the democratic process had played out. He had campaigned against Carter, but Duke respected the process more than his own personal beliefs, and he was rewarded—and surprised by—an invitation to Carter's pre-inaugural ball. At the ball, he made a memorable speech, saying: "I'm here tonight to pay my respects to our 39th president, our new commander in chief—to wish you Godspeed, sir, in the uncharted waters ahead. Tomorrow at high noon, all our hopes and dreams go into that great house with you. For you have become our transition into the unknown tomorrows, and everyone is with you. I'm pleased to be present and accounted for in this capital of freedom to witness history as it happens—to watch a common man accept the uncommon responsibility he won 'fair and square' by stating his case to the American people—not by bloodshed, beheadings and riots at the palace gates. I know I'm considered a member of the loyal opposition—accent on the loyal. I'd have it no other way."

Duke's Detective Days

By the early '70s, Duke had forever cemented himself as America's Western star and go-to action hero, having just won an Oscar for his role as the grizzled Rooster Cogburn in *True Grit* (1969). But there was more he wanted to achieve. Never one to rest on his laurels, Duke dedicated all of his considerable talent to diving headfirst into two roles often overlooked by even the most die-hard John Wayne fans: Lon McQ in *McQ* (1974) and Jim Brannigan in *Brannigan* (1975). The two urban-crime dramas marked a departure from the usual Duke fare of Westerns, war movies and the occasional romantic comedy, giving the aging actor a new outlet to showcase his undiminished charisma and charm.

For those close to John Wayne, the legend's decision to star in a modern crime movie didn't come as a shock. Duke had always had an interest in mysteries, his favorite authors being Arthur Conan Doyle and Agatha Christie. The late film critic Roger Ebert also pointed out in his review of *Brannigan* that cop and detective dramas were essentially Westerns of the modern age, featuring a similar plot structure and a clear, good-guys-versus-bad-ones dynamic. John Wayne's characters were almost always men who meant what they said, but beyond their forthright nature, there was a sincerity to them—a genuine decency that rang true for the global audience. Duke both knew about

and capitalized on that function of his acting. "All I do is sell sincerity, and I've been selling the hell out of that ever since I started," the actor said in an interview with *TIME* in 1967. His aura of honesty and authenticity made him the perfect investigative detective.

Exchanging his usual dusty locales for rainy Seattle, in Duke's first detective drama, *McQ,* he goes rogue and quits the force after most of his friends in the police department are gunned down by a mystery assassin in this neo-noir action flick. It's an interesting parallel film to another cop movie starring a Western icon released a few years earlier—*Dirty Harry* (1971) with Clint Eastwood. Both characters have to work outside the strict letter of the law to preserve what they feel is a proper moral order in the universe, pursuing wrongdoers no matter what their orders demand.

But Duke's second detective feature, *Brannigan*, played up the actor's iconic patriotism. In this 1974 film, John Wayne plays a Chicago detective whose experience with (and love for) firearms make him the indispensable man to take down an American gangster amok in London. Although Duke went back to Westerns with *Rooster Cogburn* (1975) and *The Shootist* (1976) to close out his career, the diversion into detective work was a welcome respite for fans who just wanted to see more Duke.

John Wayne brings American common sense to jolly old England in a scene from *Brannigan* (1975). The movie also starred British actor and director Richard Attenborough, brother of famous naturalist David Attenborough.

Mr. James M. Downey

President, Harvard Lampoon

I accept with pleasure your challenge to bring my new motion
picture MCQ into the pseudo-intellectual swamps of Harvard
Square.

Age, breeding and political philosophy aside, I am quite
prepared to meet nose-to-nose and fact-to-fact any or all
of the knee-jerk liberals who foul your campus.

Your intellectual pretensions, your pointy-headed radicalism ,
your Mao Tse-Tung quotations and your high-school French
proverbs could hardly pierce the hide of a man who has stormed
the Alamo, raised the flag at Iwo Jima and fought with the
Green Berets.

So comb out your beards, extinguish your pot and put a book-
marker in your Marcuse and Hesse....I'll be there on Jan. 15
for the premiere of MCQ, ready to flex muscles with the limpest
bunch of baby-brained scholars in America.

                              Sincerely,

                              JOHN WAYNE

Visiting Hostile Territory

According to the *Reading Eagle* on February 24, 1974, "The confrontation was set for January 15, at the [*Harvard*] *Lampoon*'s 44 Bow St. headquarters; the time: High Noon." Though Duke's calcified conservatism was legendary, he had agreed to debate Harvard's anti-Vietnam students who, according to a 2003 *New York Post* article by Phil Mushnick— an eyewitness to Duke's Harvard appearance— had turned the actor into "at least as much as Richard Nixon...the symbol of dim-witted and intolerant Americanism."

But the actor proved anything but thin-skinned or dim. Duke fielded questions ranging from the political ("Do you look at yourself as the fulfillment of the American Dream?") to the absurd (one student asked him if Richard Nixon would play John Wayne in the story of his life). He answered the first question with a self-deprecating quip, "I don't look at myself any more than I have to," and when a student asked about the actor's toupée he rejoined: "This is real hair! It's not mine, but it's real." The visit didn't change Duke's or the students' political views, but they discovered common ground in appreciating a good laugh.

From left: The actor's response to *The Harvard Lampoon*'s invitation; Duke made his way to Harvard Square Theater in an armored personnel carrier. After the event, photographer Ethan Boatner from the Harvard University News Office found himself face-to-face with Duke. "I asked him how he was, and he smiled and said, 'tired,'" recalls Boatner.

★ THOUGH ALL American flags deserve our respect, this one from the John Wayne Archive carries special significance: It's one of 13 flown over the Capitol building during the 1976 Bicentennial. Duke, along with select patriots such as Jesse Owens and Bob Hope, were then given these flags in recognition of their love of country. ★

Badges of Honor

All the titles, trinkets and trophies in the world won't transform a person into a patriot. That pure, honest love of country comes from years of appreciating all the freedoms and opportunities we enjoy in this great land. But it's still nice to have a symbol to show off that love to friends and neighbors. Americans knew in their bones John Wayne was one of our greatest patriots decades before the United States government decided to formally recognize Duke's tremendous contributions with a Congressional Gold Medal on the legend's 72nd birthday in 1979, mere weeks before his passing.

The medal is the highest honor Congress can bestow upon a civilian, and only a relative few have earned the honor. The legislation for giving someone the medal must be cosponsored by at least 290 members of the House of Representatives and 67 Senators before moving forward. The act of Congress put Duke in the rarefied company of men and women

The Congressional Gold Medal awarded to John Wayne for his contributions to the country, from the John Wayne Archive. The act of Congress authorized the Treasury Department to spend up to $15,000 to create the honor.

who stood tall as paragons of American bravery, imagination and innovation, such as George Washington, the Wright Brothers and Walt Disney.

In case the legislators needed any convincing of Duke's merits, a boatload of celebrities and politicians testified in front of Congress that the actor more than deserved the medal. Supporters ranged across the political spectrum, from Jimmy

John Wayne's status as a beloved American icon also prompted the U.S. Mint to cast bronze replicas of his Congressional Gold Medal, so fans and collectors could own a piece of history at the price of $3.

Other winners of the Congressional Gold Medal besides Duke (pictured center) include (clockwise from top left) Rosa Parks, Thomas Alva Edison, Walt Disney, Harry S. Truman, Bob Hope, Wilbur and Orville Wright, George Washington.

Elizabeth Taylor and Maureen O'Hara, the latter of whom appeared in five films with Duke, testify before a House subcommittee tasked with determining whether John Wayne should receive the Congressional Gold Medal, 1979.

Carter to Barry Goldwater, and Hollywood friends and colleagues such as Elizabeth Taylor, Maureen O'Hara and Kirk Douglas were among the many who urged Congress to reward Duke's lifetime of standing up for America. John Wayne himself couldn't speak on his own behalf, as he was in the final stages of his battle with cancer, but the outpouring of support (and simple common sense) convinced Congress to pass the act on May 26, 1979.

Duke didn't live to receive the medal signifying a nation's gratitude toward its biggest and most beloved hero. In March 1980, President Jimmy Carter presented John Wayne's family the medal, inscribed with the words "John Wayne—American." A few months later, Carter would posthumously bestow upon the icon the Presidential Medal of Freedom—an honor started by President Harry Truman to recognize the monumental contributions to advancing freedom and human dignity—something Duke did every day through the way he walked, talked and lived.

John Wayne in *The Sons of Katie Elder* (1965), the first film he made after undergoing cancer treatment and having a lung removed the year before.

★1979–Now★
STILL FIGHTING

THOUGH JOHN WAYNE has been gone for decades—he passed on June 11, 1979, after battling cancer on and off for the previous 15 years—his legacy is as strong as ever. After more than 50 years of making movies, speaking his mind, honoring our troops and proudly declaring himself a patriot, John Wayne had effectively woven himself into the fabric of America, becoming a permanent part of the country's culture and history. It's safe to say he would be proud of this well-earned place: Duke loved his country more than just about anything, and to him, that was the way it should be. As he put it, "I am an old-fashioned, honest-to-goodness, flag-waving patriot." So it's only fitting that when modern Americans think of the entertainers who did the most to foster an image worthy of the American Dream, John Wayne often comes to mind first.

John Wayne sits with his son Ethan, who was named for Duke's character in *The Searchers* (1956).

But in the way he lived his life, Duke was just as much of an enduring American icon for those who shared his flag-waving patriotism as the characters he played on-screen. Whether it meant speaking up when he disagreed, supporting the troops when they needed it most, or telling a story he felt needed to be told, John Wayne's patriotism was unwavering, and always came from a place of the deepest respect for the values of the Constitution. He even put his love of the U.S. on wax, recording the spoken word album *America, Why I Love Her*. Duke is so associated with the idea of rugged individualism and the American way that the Army's standard issue multi-purpose can opener, the P-38, is colloquially known as "John Wayne" because of its ability to prove useful in tricky or unexpected situations.

It was this larger-than-life version of Americana that endeared Duke to millions, and it was also one that would, in its own way, come to define the decade following his death. As Jimmy Carter's defeat in the 1980 election would show, the trend of 1970s liberalism was giving way to a throwback conservatism exemplified by Ronald Reagan. Where many saw Carter as representing a weakening of the American position on the world stage, Reagan promised a proactive approach to ending the threat of communism. And where many had trepidation at the idea of too much change too fast, Reagan was happy to encourage a return to 1950s style values. It's his style of conservatism, based on the principles John Wayne embraced most dearly, that would predominate among conservatives for the next three decades.

In his films, Duke gave us the most enduring image of the all-American Western hero: someone who is able to deal with whatever problems might arise through his own skill and will power. "John Wayne was bigger than life," said President Jimmy Carter upon Duke's passing. "In an age of few heroes, he was the genuine article." The president was correct: John Wayne was bigger than life. Whether it's Rooster Cogburn's eyepatch, J.B. Books holding his own until the very end or Colonel Mike Kirby proclaiming "Out here, due process is a bullet," just about every American has a favorite John Wayne memory. The legend's career has far outlasted his lifetime, broadcasting a strong, determined, courageous symbol of America to the rest of the world.

John Wayne's family poses for the unveiling of a bronze statue commemorating his legacy at Western Plaza in Beverly Hills, 1984. At the time of his death, Duke had 21 grandchildren.

Lady of the Ranch

While Duke's influence on the film industry is an obvious fact, the actor influenced America's history far beyond the cinema. One unexpected arena where John Wayne's presence is still felt today is in animal husbandry, a kinder and gentler industry thanks in part to America's favorite on-screen cowboy.

The state of the cattle industry in the 1970s was, from a modern viewpoint, often appalling. "There was a tremendous amount of rough, cruel handling of cattle," says Dr. Temple Grandin, a world-renowned expert in animal science and livestock management. Grandin, who started working at feedyards in 1970s Arizona, says she routinely witnessed workers shocking cattle with electrified prods repeatedly, killing animals by jacking up the hydraulic pressure in cattle chutes and, in one instance, breaking a calf's neck while wrestling with it. But for Grandin, who credits her unique visual imagination with allowing her to see the world through an animal's eyes, took a different approach, one that revolutionized the relationship between the herder and the herd.

Grandin started that revolution with her design of a dip vat at an Arizona feedyard in '76. Before Grandin, ranch hands forced the terrified cattle to walk, jam-packed, down a concrete slope to submerge themselves in a 7-foot-deep pool of insecticide and then emerge on the other side. It was dangerous, and often deadly, for the cattle. Grandin designed a more gradual concrete decline with grooves over its surface, which made the process safer for the animals.

Grandin's ideas found slow acceptance among the hardened cowboys who had been raising cattle for generations. "I think a lot of the pushback was because I was a girl going into a man's industry," Grandin says. One place more accepting was John Wayne's Red River Feedyard, which she joined in '78. "It was a

Dr. Temple Grandin speaks outside of the U.S. Patent and Trademark Office (USPTO) on April 3, 2016, in Denver, Colorado. Grandin has autism and was able to excel in her profession despite a general lack of understanding of her condition through a tenacious attitude even Duke would be proud of.

dream job," she says. "Ted Gilbert, who was in charge of the feedyard, was a wonderful man and a mentor." Gilbert and the others hired Grandin to replicate the success of her previous dip vat at Duke's feedyard, which managed 83,000 head of cattle at any given time. Grandin recalls meeting the actor once at a cattle sale. "He signed my bull program," she says. "He just seemed like a nice, old, big cowboy guy."

Today, Grandin's principles of providing cattle with a low-stress environment have become the new standard. "There's a lot of interest in not yelling at the cattle while handling them, moving them in small groups and being quiet while working with them," says Grandin. "When I first started talking about those things, in the '70s and '80s, I was laughed at. Now, people take it seriously."

Perfect Pair

John Wayne may have defined the Western with the scores of films he made during a 50-year career, but his legacy doesn't end there. Thanks to Duke, the Western still thrives as an essential American artform, as evidenced by the following modern classics in the genre.

DANCES WITH WOLVES (1990)
Influenced by Hondo *(1953)*

When *Dances with Wolves* opened in theaters in November of 1990, the Western genre wasn't dead, but audiences could be forgiven for planning its funeral. Movies exploring the exploits of cowboys and gunslingers only appeared sporadically at the cinema and had been pushed out of the cultural limelight by more bombastic action movies that seemed to better capture the high-adrenaline spirit of the late 20th century. What more did stories set in the dusty Old West have left to say?

Quite a bit, it turns out. Director and star Kevin Costner leveraged his (at-the-time) considerable star power to create his three-

From top: A poster for the movie *Hondo*; Kevin Costner in a scene from *Dances with Wolves* (1990).

hour Western epic. Despite the striking scenes the film presents showcasing the beauty of the Western frontier, the most memorable and audacious part of the movie was its focus on one man's spiritual journey from disillusioned soldier to member of a Lakota Sioux tribe. While many audiences and critics rightly lauded *Dances with Wolves* for its sympathetic portrayal of a people who often served as stock villains in the Westerns of the past, one of Duke's own classics dipped at least a few toes in the same pond—the 1953 film *Hondo*.

The John Wayne film, similar to Costner's later masterpiece, recontextualizes the role of Native Americans in the Western. Although many of the Apaches in the film serve as antagonists threatening the lives of Hondo and those near and dear to him, most of them are treated as dangerous warriors defending their way of life against a government that has repeatedly broken its word to them. It may not be as revolutionary as casting the white expansionists as out-and-out villains as *Dances with Wolves* does, but Hondo's sympathies can be seen as the start of a journey Costner finished with his modern classic.

UNFORGIVEN (1992)
Influenced by* Angel and the Badman *(1947)

One of the boldest Westerns made in the history of the genre, *Unforgiven*, challenges most of the assumptions underpinning the classic Westerns of the past—including many starring John Wayne. *Unforgiven* stars Clint Eastwood (who also directed the film) as William Munny, a former bloodthirsty outlaw who has since forsworn

his life of violence for domestic bliss on the farm. Enticed to join a young hothead hunting a bounty for a sizable reward, Munny nevertheless spends most of the movie acting timid and out-of-practice, a far cry from the ruthless killer of his reputation.

The idea of the outlaw trying to turn over a new leaf was a plot tackled decades before *Unforgiven* by the John Wayne movie *Angel and the Badman* (1947). The film stars Duke as Quirt Evans, a gunman who finds himself in the care of Quakers, whose pacifist lifestyle begins influencing Evans's own. *Angel and the Badman* and *Unforgiven* may share a similar premise, but the films give very different answers to the question of whether violence can ever be moral. In *Angel and the Badman*, Quirt is saved from having to dispatch the movie's heavy himself by the intervention of the local marshal. *Unforgiven*'s William Munny, however, goes on a killing spree against those who wronged him (including the local sheriff and his deputies), riding off into the night with fresh sins to regret.

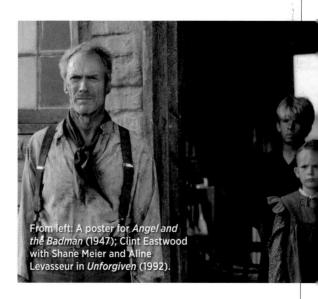

From left: A poster for *Angel and the Badman* (1947); Clint Eastwood with Shane Meier and Aline Levasseur in *Unforgiven* (1992).

From top: Val Kilmer, Sam Elliott, Kurt Russell and Bill Paxton in a scene from *Tombstone* (1993); a poster for *Rio Bravo* (1959).

TOMBSTONE (1993)
Influenced by Rio Bravo *(1959)*

The Western genre has endured in large part because the films often address heavy and weighty themes about America, civilization and progress. But Westerns have also stuck around because it's fun to watch stories of lawmen and outlaws facing off against each other. Maybe no other modern Western has nailed the feeling of pure entertainment found in the best of John Wayne's movies than the 1993 movie *Tombstone*. Starring Kurt Russell as famed (former) lawman Wyatt Earp and featuring superb supporting performances from Val Kilmer, Powers Boothe, Sam Elliott, Bill Paxton and more, this endlessly rewatchable retelling of the Earp clan's fate leading up to the gunfight at the O.K. Corral and beyond feels like it would be a favorite of Duke's had he been around to enjoy it.

While John Wayne never starred in a film depicting the historical events covered in *Tombstone*, the movie in his filmography it closely resembles is *Rio Bravo* (1959). The plot of both films share similar beats involving a lawman and his dedicated posse of friends going after the bad guys despite overwhelming odds against them. But the real way in which *Rio Bravo* reveals itself as a direct influence on *Tombstone* is the tension both Westerns pack into every minute of runtime. Whether watching Johnny Ringo and Doc Holliday threaten each other in Latin over a card game or Sheriff John T. Chance round up a bar full of suspects in a search for an attempted assassin, audiences find plenty of reasons to come back to both of these Western masterpieces.

THE ASSASSINATION OF JESSE JAMES BY THE COWARD ROBERT FORD (2007)

Influenced by* The Shootist *(1976)

A meditative Western covering the downfall of the James-Younger Gang and focusing on the distance between myth and reality, this 2007 Western shouldn't be anyone's first pick for a feel-good flick. But in addition to the stunning cinematography, the movie rewards its viewer with outstanding performances from Brad Pitt and Casey Affleck as Jesse James and his killer Robert Ford, respectively, in a story that sticks around long after the credits roll.

The Assassination of Jesse James addresses the always-evergreen questions of what constitutes honorable behavior and what sort of legacy we want to leave behind.

Audiences of John Wayne's last film, *The Shootist* (1976), also find themselves pondering similar questions when watching Duke's melancholy send-off. The story of a dying gunfighter who reckons with his own past while disabusing a young man (played by Ron Howard) of his lifestyle's appeal, *The Shootist* sees the Western's greatest icon wrestle with one of his greatest acting challenges yet—and succeed. Both *The Shootist* and *The Assassination of Jesse James* illustrate the beautiful melancholy of a good ending, and how legends don't have to happily ride off into the sunset in order to win the day.

From top: A poster for *The Shootist* (1976); Casey Affleck and Brad Pitt in a scene from *The Assassination of Jesse James by the Coward Robert Ford* (2007).

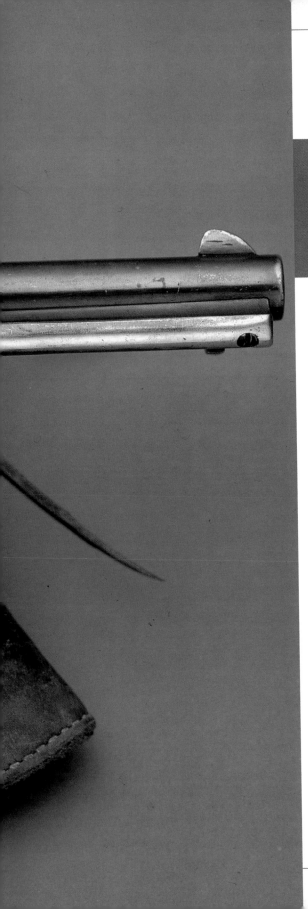

Remembering our Heritage

John Wayne spent a career protecting the peace and defending the weak on the silver screen, wielding some of the most iconic weapons of the Old West. Duke understood the tools of his trade were more than just Hollywood props: They were pieces of history. And like all items of cultural importance, they belonged in a museum. In this case, John Wayne felt the best home for some of his firearms was the Cowboy Hall of Fame in Oklahoma City, Oklahoma (known today as the National Cowboy & Western Heritage Museum). Along with his personal collection of Western art and memorabilia, Duke gifted the National Cowboy & Western Heritage Museum 63 guns, knives and other assorted weapons after his death in 1979. The donation was a sign of trust between cinema's greatest cowboy and the institution dedicated to the great American West. John Wayne had been on the museum's board of trustees for more than 10 years, and was marshal of the parade celebrating its opening in 1955. This Colt Model 1873 Single Action Army Revolver (pictured left) and the Winchester Model 1892 rifle (with a custom loop lever, and used in *True Grit*, below) remain on display at the museum for all to view and appreciate.

From left: The interior of the National Cowboy & Western Heritage Museum. More than 10 million visitors total have come to the museum to see the 28,000 plus pieces of Western art and artifacts; this 8'8" bronze statue of Duke stands larger than life at the museum. The piece was created by Edward J. Fraughton and was unveiled to the public in 2007.

The House that Duke Built

Most of the rough-and-tumble cowboys Duke brought to life on the silver screen didn't seem like the type to spend an afternoon wandering the halls of a museum. But the National Cowboy & Western Heritage Museum in Oklahoma City caters to a different kind of visitor. Hoping to attract people more interested in saddles and six-shooters than postmodern paintings, the museum boasts an impressive collection of artifacts tracing the history of the cowboy since the days of the conquistadors. And John Wayne, the man most responsible for the popularization of the cowboy mythos in America, pitched in to give the fledgling museum his blessing right from the beginning in the 1960s.

Driven by a love for all things Western, the acting legend played a pivotal role in helping what was originally named the Cowboy Hall of Fame grow into the country's foremost authority on and protector of Western culture. Duke provided seed money needed for the organizers to erect a permanent home for cowboy culture, and, when construction began in 1960, the actor also lent his celebrity at a public event. Traveling to Oklahoma, Duke branded a "W" into a wooden concrete form. When the museum was ready for the public five years later, John Wayne led a parade through downtown Oklahoma City as part of a weekend of festivities celebrating the vitality and vigor of the American West. Governors or representatives of the museum's 17 member-states took part in a flag-raising ceremony, and members of various Native American tribes performed a ceremonial dance to bless the institute, underscoring the museum's dedication to representing the rich cultural diversity of the American West.

Duke's dedication didn't waver as the years wore on, and the actor proudly served on the museum's board of directors until he passed away in 1979. He left the museum his collection of movie memorabilia, firearms and artwork, including 68 kachina dolls. Today, the assemblage stands for visitors to enjoy, a living legacy of Duke's love for Western culture.

Inspired to Heal

One of the reasons Duke remains such a beloved icon to all Americans is because his characters always threw themselves into the toughest fights, doing whatever it took to get the job done. In 1981, his eldest son Michael fulfilled one of John Wayne's last wishes by lending the legend's name to the John Wayne Cancer Clinic. The Clinic partnered with Saint John's Health Center to open the John Wayne Cancer Institute in Santa Monica, California, in 1991. Since then, it has helped push the boundaries of research into treating cancer, training top-rate surgical oncologists through its fellowship program. Three of that program's alumni—Dr. Anthony Lucci, Professor of Surgery in the departments of Surgical Oncology and Breast Surgical Oncology at The University of Texas MD Anderson Cancer Center; Dr. Mark Faries, head of surgical oncology and co-director of the melanoma program at the Angeles Clinic and Research Institute in Los Angeles; and Dr. Terry Sarantou, surgical oncologist, academic faculty member at the Levine Cancer Institute and member of North Carolina's Commission on Cancer—talk about how the legacy of John Wayne inspires their work.

What makes the training you received at the JWCI Fellowship stand out from training you could receive elsewhere?
LUCCI We were fortunate during our fellowship at JWCI to work with leaders such as Dr. Donald Morton [John Wayne's head physician during the actor's treatment] and Dr. Armando Giuliano. These outstanding clinicians also happened to be innovators, whose work has changed how we practice surgical oncology today. We were fortunate to be able to work with them on a daily basis in the clinics and the operating room.

FARIES The direct contact with legends such as Don Morton and the ability to collaborate closely with them in the clinic and in research was a unique opportunity. Even in other institutions with world-renowned surgeons, fellows are kept at something of a distance. At JWCI, we were all part of the family.

SARANTOU Training at the John Wayne Cancer Institute was unique because of the culture that existed, which fostered innovative thinking, the ability to challenge the status quo and fostered collaboration beyond traditional

John Wayne in *Red River* (1948). The actor would have his first brush with cancer 15 years later, but doctors were able to successfully remove the tumor from his lung.

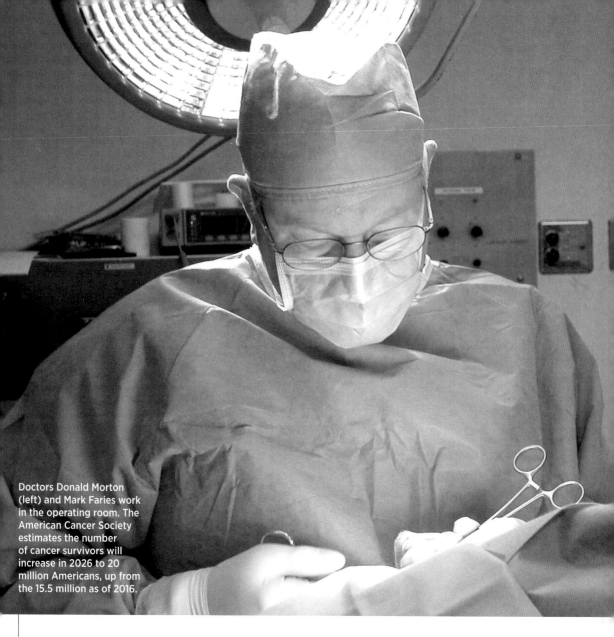

Doctors Donald Morton (left) and Mark Faries work in the operating room. The American Cancer Society estimates the number of cancer survivors will increase in 2026 to 20 million Americans, up from the 15.5 million as of 2016.

surgical training. Dr. Morton repeatedly told me to "keep dreaming."

What's been the most significant gain the medical community has made in treating cancer since John Wayne's death in 1979?
LUCCI There is obviously much more hope when we talk to cancer patients about their diagnosis. Today, a patient with a HER2-amplified breast cancer will be given great hope knowing that in 2017 we have extremely effective targeted agents to treat

their disease. This simply wasn't the case in 1979. The same holds true for many other cancers—there are so many more options for effective treatment today.

FARIES We live in a new world. Cancer treatment has been revolutionized on three fronts: technology, genomics and immunology. Technology allows us to perform operations more safely and effectively in minimally invasive approaches, speeding recovery and reducing complications. Genomics, studying

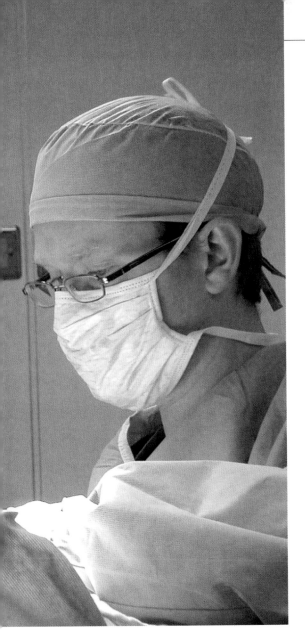

SARANTOU Dr. Morton had the foresight to understand that many cancers are due to changes in a patient's immune system. He was way ahead of his time and led the research to look at fighting cancers by altering the immune system. If he were alive today, he would be pleased to see the ideas he envisioned being used to develop exciting immunotherapies available for treating melanoma.

How does the John Wayne legacy of determination and perseverance apply to the fight against cancer?
SARANTOU With grit and tenacity, the John Wayne legacy continues in the development of innovative surgical techniques and new medical therapies.

FARIES Despite the recent progress we've made, cancer remains a terrifying diagnosis. I'm sure it is tempting in the face of a serious diagnosis to try to hide or avoid the challenges of treatment. But as John Wayne said about courage, we might be scared to death, but we need to "saddle up anyway." It is through the courage and determination of patients who were willing to take a chance and enroll in a clinical trial that we have made the progress we've enjoyed over the recent past. It will take more of the same courage to keep that progress rolling.

a tumor's DNA and RNA, have allowed the development of what are called targeted therapies. These can be more effective than older drugs such as chemotherapy, with fewer side effects. The biggest revolution, though, is in [the] use of the immune system to fight cancer. Don Morton was one of the original pioneers in this area, and it is now radically changing the way many cancers are treated. One great thing about these immune therapies is that when they work, they can work for very long periods of time, possibly forever.

LUCCI I think we all know that this fight is difficult. Even though we have made progress and improved outcomes for many cancers, there is still much work to be done. I don't think any of us will be satisfied until we drop the death rate from cancer even more.

★ THE IMAGE OF DUKE riding away at the end of *True Grit* (1969) is a favorite for many Americans. Almost four decades after his death, John Wayne remains one of America's best-loved movie stars—and research firm Harris Insights and Analytics has the numbers to prove it. According to the Harris Poll, one of the longest running surveys of public opinion, John Wayne is still one of America's top 5 favorite actors. Duke ranked 4th in the 2016 poll, and was the only actor of the top 10 who was not still making movies. Perhaps even more impressively, John Wayne is the only actor to have consistently appeared in the list's top 10 actors for more than two decades. Ethan Wayne is not surprised at his father's longevity, however. "John Wayne was more than just a movie star, he was an American icon," he explained. "His personality on- and offscreen embodied honorable virtues that continue to resonate with the American people today. We are proud that he remains an emblem of all that it means to be not only a good citizen, but a good person." ★

Media Lab Books
For inquiries, call 646-838-6637

Copyright 2018 Topix Media Lab

Published by Topix Media Lab
14 Wall Street, Suite 4B
New York, NY 10005

Printed in USA

ISBN-10: 0-9987898-2-8
ISBN-13: 978-0-9987898-2-8

CEO Tony Romando

Vice President and Publisher Phil Sexton
Vice President of Sales and New Markets Tom Mifsud
Vice President of Brand Marketing Joy Bomba
Vice President of Retail Sales & Logistics Linda Greenblatt
Director of Finance Vandana Patel
Manufacturing Director Nancy Puskuldjian
Financial Analyst Matthew Quinn
Brand Marketing Assistant Taylor Hamilton

Editor-in-Chief Jeff Ashworth
Creative Director Steven Charny
Photo Director Dave Weiss
Managing Editor Courtney Kerrigan
Senior Editor Tim Baker

Content Editors James Ellis, Kaytie Norman
Content Designer Michelle Lock
Art Director Susan Dazzo
Associate Art Director Rebecca Stone
Assistant Managing Editor Holland Baker
Designer Danielle Santucci
Assistant Photo Editors Catherine Armanasco, Stephanie Jones
Assistant Editor Alicia Kort
Editorial Assistants Courtney Henderson-Adams, Sean Romano

Co-Founders Bob Lee, Tony Romando